CYCLING *without* TRAFFIC: WALES

DIAL HOUSE

John Price

First published 1999

ISBN 0 7110 2645 9

© John Price 1999

Published by Dial House

an imprint of Ian Allan Publishing Ltd,
Terminal House, Shepperton,
Surrey TW17 8AS.
Printed by Ian Allan Printing Ltd,
Riverdene Business Park,
Hersham, Surrey KT12 4RG.

The right of John Price to be identified
as Author of this Work has been
asserted by him in accordance with
the Copyright, Designs & Patents Act,
1988.

Code: 9903/E

Front cover, main picture: A steep section of the
Monmouthshire & Brecon Canal towpath,

Front cover, inset: Checking the map on the Lôn
Eifion Cycleway.

Previous page: Downhill stretch at Coed y Brenin
Forest Park.

This page: On the trail alongside Garreg-ddu
Reservoir.

CONTENTS 🚲 3

As I sit here in the Afan Valley on an October day, looking down upon the river, with the autumn leaves forming a carpet over the cycleway, my mind turns back to early April when we undertook the first ride on the Taff Trail, with snow still on the tops of the Brecon Beacons north of Merthyr. I realise that it has indeed been a very pleasant summer exploring this small principality of Wales, and hunting out the best places to enjoy peaceful, relaxed and traffic-free cycling.

In a way, the Afan Valley typifies what makes Wales so special from the cyclist's viewpoint. Like most of the valleys in South Wales, the industrial activity of previous years has provided a railway line which is now disused and provides an excellent basis for a cycle path. But the Afan Valley is fortunate enough to be blessed with another traffic-free route on the other side of the river, making a circular route possible. Gone are the pit wheel and the scars produced by mining — the uninitiated would not know they had ever been there. All that is left is a beautiful valley waiting to be cycled.

I must make it clear that this book is written for 'potterers' who wish to spend a relaxing day cycling at no particular pace. It is also written with the family in mind, who may be intending to take a holiday touring Wales and who would like to take their bikes with them. The book describes 30 rides in detail covering 368 miles of cycling on old railway lines, on canal towpaths, around reservoirs and thorough forests. It contains background information on places of interest on the rides or nearby, and in addition it contains a wealth of material on all cycling opportunities in the area with the addresses of organisations that can provide further information.

And as for the weather in so-called 'Wild Wales' — well, in the generally indifferent British summer of 1998, it turned out to be much better than I expected. Yes, it was capricious and it changed at a moment's notice, but only three days could be described as thoroughly wet.

Finally, Sustrans' plans for the National Cycle Network are proceeding apace with 3,000 miles of the network due for completion by Midsummer's Day in 2000. Many of the rides in this book are the traffic-free sections of either National Route 8 (Lôn Las Cymru) from Chepstow/Cardiff to Holyhead, or they form part of the proposed National Route 4 (Celtic Trail) from Newport to Kidwelly. In my contacts with the many authorities involved, it is clear that the network is stimulating a great deal of activity and over the next few years many additional routes intended to feed the national routes will become available. So, we cyclists are about to enter a golden age, but in the meantime there are already many miles of extremely pleasant cycling just waiting to be discovered with the help of this book.

Above: A pause by the River Taff.

Below: Cader Idris, near Dolgellau.

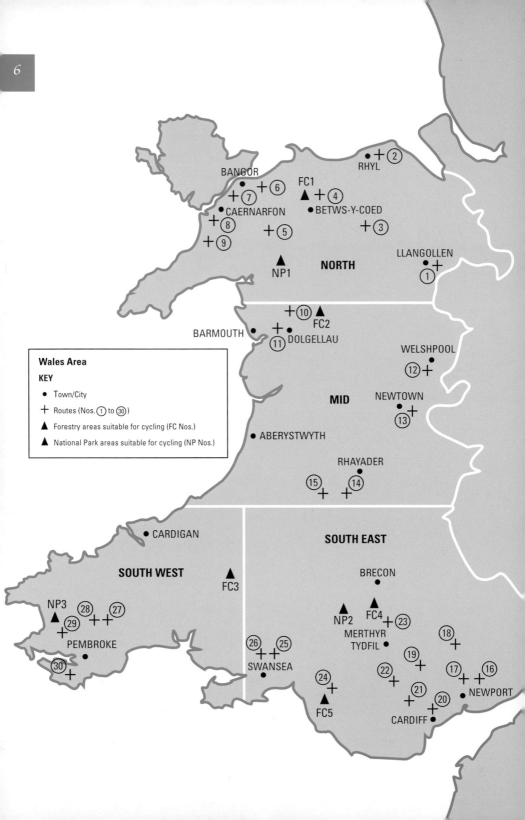

Wales Area

KEY

● Town/City

+ Routes (Nos. ① to ㉚)

▲ Forestry areas suitable for cycling (FC Nos.)

▲ National Park areas suitable for cycling (NP Nos.)

RHYL

BANGOR

FC1

②

⑥

⑦

④

BETWS-Y-COED

CAERNARFON

⑧

⑤

③

⑨

LLANGOLLEN

NP1

NORTH

①

⑩

FC2

BARMOUTH

⑪

DOLGELLAU

WELSHPOOL

⑫

MID

NEWTOWN

⑬

ABERYSTWYTH

RHAYADER

⑮

⑭

CARDIGAN

SOUTH EAST

SOUTH WEST

FC3

BRECON

NP3

⑱

㉗

㉘

NP2

FC4

㉙

㉓

PEMBROKE

MERTHYR

TYDFIL

㉖

㉕

⑲

㉚

SWANSEA

⑰

⑯

⑯

㉔

㉒

NEWPORT

㉑

⑳

FC5

CARDIFF

Acknowledgements

On a personal note I would like to thank my wife Veronica for her considerable contribution as 'logistics support officer' and proof-reader, and for her company on many rides; and also my son Christopher for his support and company on several rides. I am also grateful for the information provided by Sustrans, the CTC, the Wales Tourist Board and the many authorities involved with the development of cycling in Wales.

Picture Credits

All uncredited photographs are by the author.
Maps by RS Illustrations, Liss, Hants.

Background Sources

The author wishes to mention the following books as having been particularly valuable for reference and background: *The Blue Guide to Wales* by John Tomes (A. & C. Black); *Exploring Wales* by William Condry (Faber & Faber); *In Search of Wales* by H. V. Morton (Methuen & Co); *Highways and Byways in North Wales* by A. G. Bradley (Macmillan & Co); *Highways and Byways in South Wales* by A. G. Bradley (Macmillan & Co); *Wild Wales* by George Borrow (Collins).

Above: Cycling on the Brunel Cycle Track.

The aim of this book is to supply the ideas and information that a family needs to enjoy a day of completely safe cycling in Wales. Information has been obtained from many sources including Sustrans, the British Waterways Board, the Forestry Commission, Welsh Water and the unitary authorities. Cycling opportunities can be broken down into the following categories.

DISMANTLED RAILWAYS

These are ideal for family cycling as they are usually flat, ideally surfaced and well drained. Many are almost entirely intact like the Lôn Eifion Route in Caernarfon and the Mawddach Trail near Dolgellau, and virtually uninterrupted cycling can be enjoyed for many miles, but others have had their bridges removed which can make a dismantled railway ride frustratingly hard work. If you study an Ordnance Survey map you will see many dismantled railway routes that could have been made into cycle trails — these could have formed a ready-made national cycle network. The loss of these routes, largely during the 'Beeching cuts' was such a short-sighted policy. Many of them have now been built on, or their course extinguished and beyond recovery.

CANAL TOWPATHS

Canal towpaths are excellent for cycling as they provide a flat route, there is always something going on in a peaceful sort of way, and there is an abundance of flora and fauna. Unfortunately, the surface of the towpaths can be changeable and vary from tarmac to mud. The number of canals in Wales is limited and there are basically four of note — the Llangollen, the Montgomery, the Monmouthshire & Brecon, and the Swansea Canal. Cycling on most of these is fully covered in the main part of this book. A free permit is currently required for cycling the Llangollen and Montgomery Canals and this is obtainable from British Waterways' Ellesmere Office (Tel: 01691 622549).

FORESTRY COMMISSION LAND

Cycling is encouraged on most tracts of land owned or managed by the Forestry Commission. In Wales we are fortunate to have many miles of possible traffic-free cycling opportunities on good forestry roads, with a number of excellently waymarked trails, where it is virtually impossible to go wrong. The section on Forestry Commission Land, National Parks and Welsh Water provides further information.

CYCLING ON QUIET ROADS AND RIGHTS OF WAY

I often prefer to cycle part of a route on quiet country roads as they take you through our beautiful villages, which a railway or canal-based route might very well bypass. Some of the routes in this book are based on a traffic-free route but also suggest a return leg on a

quiet country lane. An example is Route 18 where the outward leg is via the Monmouthshire & Brecon Canal and the return is via quiet country lanes in the Usk Valley. If you wish to enjoy the increased range of cycling that can be obtained by considering quiet lanes, then many of the county and district councils produce recommended routes in their own areas. Examples are the 'Conwy Valley Cycle Route' and 'Rural Cycling in Anglesey'. Details of many of these routes and points of contact for more information are contained in the chapter 'Routes Described in Local Authority Leaflets'. Alternatively, if you enjoy maps then why not plan a route for yourself? An Ordnance Survey Landranger map (1:50,000 scale) is the best for this. It will not take you much time to learn how to identify which of the 'yellow' roads are best for cycling. One fairly serious shortcoming of Ordnance Survey maps is the situation with 'white'

roads. These are roads or tracks where it is impossible to tell from the map whether the public has access or not. Thankfully, the Ordnance Survey are now starting to improve this situation on their new series of Explorer Maps (1:25,000 scale). Finally, you can of course cycle on bridleways (but you must give way to horse riders and pedestrians), Roads Used as Public Paths (RUPPs) and Byways Open to All Traffic (BOATs). Although traffic may be free to use the latter classifications, it is fairly rare to encounter a vehicle, but the surface can be expected to be very variable. The incidence of these rights of way that are usable by cyclists varies considerably due to the topography of each county.

Below: There are good views alongside the Taff Trail.

The completion of a National Cycle Network has been the aim of Sustrans for 18 years and the project received a tremendous boost by obtaining funding of £42 million in 1995 from the Millennium Commission from National Lottery funds. Sustrans planned to complete the first 2,500 miles by June 2000, with the remaining 4,000 miles due to be completed by 2005. Work is ahead of schedule, with progress by June 2000 now expected to be 3,000 miles. Although the project is led by Sustrans, it is a partnership with over 400 local authorities and landowning bodies, government departments and specialist and local interest groups. It will consist of approximately 50% traffic-free sections with the remainder on segregated or traffic-calmed roads. A fundamental design aim is that the whole network will be safe for use by a sensible, unsupervised 12 year old. During the compilation of this book, I became very aware of the impact that the National Cycle Network is having in Wales. Many of the traffic-free routes in this book are component parts of either National Route 8 (Lôn Las Cymru) from Chepstow/Cardiff to Holyhead, or the proposed National Route 4 (Celtic Way) that will run from Newport to Kidwelly. The development of feeder routes to the National Cycle Network, especially in the Valleys, means that in the next couple of years several new traffic-free routes will be made available.

Above: Time to talk on the cycle path.

THE BICYCLE

Broadly there are four basic types of bike available in the shops today that would be suitable for the potterer. Starting with the least sophisticated, there is the traditional sit-up-and-beg three-speed roadster, favoured by vicars, and students in Oxford and Cambridge, but not really for serious consideration here. Then there is the touring bike, characterised by its drop handlebars and racks for carrying panniers. The mountain bike has in recent years become very popular because of its ability to go anywhere, and it can now be bought with front and rear suspension, although this is not necessary for the rides in this book. Finally, there is the hybrid which looks like a mountain bike but has smaller diameter wheels and thinner tyres, so you get the advantage of the robustness of a mountain bike with greater speed. All of the rides classified as easy in this book could be undertaken on all four types, but the moderate or demanding ones would make a mountain or hybrid desirable. If you are not certain of the cycle that you wish to buy, try hiring one first. Then when you have tried cycling and you find that it is enjoyable, go to a small shop that specialises in cycling and seek advice.

HELMET AND HEADGEAR

The potterer should wear a helmet if he or she is able to and should also try to ensure that children wear one. Having said that, even the modern lightweight ventilated ones are very uncomfortable and inconvenient on a hot day when sweat drips into your eyes. If you really cannot bring yourself to wear a helmet at certain times, comfort yourself with the thought that the health and fitness benefits of cycling are considerably greater than the actual chance of a serious head injury. As far as children are concerned, the risk of a serious head injury is only about a third of the risk of a child experiencing a head injury from climbing or jumping. Nevertheless, helmets offer a limited but significant amount of protection to the skull and brain if you fall

off and hit your head on the ground. If you are not wearing a helmet in cold weather, you should always wear a hat as it will save a significant amount of heat loss.

CLOTHES

To wear, or not to wear, a pair of those infamous brightly coloured, body-hugging lycra cycling shorts for the first time is a big decision in the potterer's life. On the one hand they are a trifle over the top for pottering, and they show up all bulges, but they can be a real blessing. Cycle shorts wear well, do not have seams in the wrong places and are lined with chamois which sticks to your skin and prevents abrasion. Track suit trousers or jogging suits are a good alternative but they need to be fairly tight fitting. There are specialist cycling tracksuits which have zip legs and high backs, but ordinary tracksuit bottoms should suffice. Jeans are not a particularly good idea. They have large seams in the wrong places and are too stiff and cold when wet.

One of the least practical items for day-long rides are cycle clips. If you like to wear ordinary trousers, and want to keep your self respect by not tucking your trousers into your navy blue socks, then turn up the trouser leg a few inches. This looks acceptable especially with white socks or bare brown legs.

On the upper half of the body it is best to follow the well-established layer principle, taking with you several layers of clothing rather than a single thick item, and peeling off or putting on as required.

As far as weather is concerned, it is very advisable to listen to a weather forecast before you decide to go cycling and that way you can avoid the worst soaking. If you do cycle in the rain, no matter what you wear, you will find yourself getting clammy and probably wet anyway, due to the waterproof garment not 'breathing' fast enough to rid it of perspiration, despite the claims of many manufacturers. The old-fashioned cape can be very good as it allows plenty of circulation of air. If you take waterproofs, you will need to consider how you are going to carry them. A rucksack is feasible, but a better idea is a set of front or rear panniers, with the latter probably being the best. These avoid a sweaty back and have a low centre of gravity. If you think big and go for a large set of panniers, these could suffice for the whole family.

FOOTWEAR

There are sophisticated pedal and shoe systems which attach the shoe to the pedal. The shoe has a plate that locates into the pedal and will release from the pedal by twisting the foot sideways. But they are a bit specialist for the potterer and for the purposes of this book, trainers are likely to be the best bet.

WHAT TO TAKE

There is a minimal amount of kit that you need to take to stand you in good stead for most eventualities. The biggest worry is, of course, a puncture. To counter this you should ensure that you carry a pump with flexible connectors suitable for the range of tyre valves that you and your group may be using. I always carry both a puncture repair kit (the Cure-C-Cure type are best) and a spare inner tube, on the grounds that if you are unable to repair a flat tyre your day out will be ruined. To accompany these, a set of three tyre levers are essential and an adjustable spanner with a capacity of up to about 25mm. In the heat of summer it is important to remember to take sufficient drink to last you all day, so that you avoid becoming dehydrated. You should also consider the best way to carry this guide book or your map. You could use a handlebar-mounted bag, which often has a clear pocket on top, or obtain a handlebar map carrier, which is rare but very practical. Alternatively, you could use a walker's map carrier, slung over your back. This sounds unlikely, but works quite well in practice. The minimal kit list that a wise family ought to consider taking should therefore include:

- waterproofs
- a pump with appropriate connectors
- a puncture repair kit
- a spare inner tube
- a set of tyre levers
- an adjustable spanner
- a small screwdriver
- a spray can of cycle oil
- spare jumpers
- gloves (for winter, spring and autumn)
- a lock
- a rag or some 'wipes' to clean your hands after a repair
- cycle bottles
- a map carrier or equivalent
- a small rucksack or pannier bag

Finally, the instructions given in the rides are recorded at specific distances. An inexpensive cycle computer would therefore be a useful aid. This is not a book on bicycle maintenance but

Below: Taff Trail mosaic plaque at Merthyr Tydfil.

it is important to carry out certain checks before a ride. Checking for faults after a ride is even better as it will mean that you are much more likely to have the time to sort the problem out properly. This section concentrates on safety-critical checks which can be divided into three categories:

BRAKE CHECKS

Squeeze the brake lever and check that the brake blocks touch the rim after moving the lever between 1cm and 2cm from the rest position. If less, that is OK provided the rim does not rub against the block and make your cycling hard work. If the movement is greater than 2cm then the brakes need adjusting. Brake cables tend to deteriorate through neglect so these need to be inspected regularly. If the cable is frayed or seriously rusty it should be replaced immediately. Inspect brake blocks and ensure that there is plenty of material left, indicated by the depth of the water-dispersing grooves. Better quality blocks have indicator lines which show the maximum wear limit. One of the most common and annoying problems that occurs with cycle brakes blocks is squealing. This is easily solved in most cases by repositioning the blocks so that they take up a slightly 'toe-in' position.

TYRE CHECKS

The rides in this book are not particularly demanding so the requirement is to have tyres which are properly inflated and have a full coverage of tread with no damaged sections. Mountain bike tyres will perform best if their pressure is varied according to anticipated use. Optimum grip for off-road use requires a lower pressure than minimum rolling resistance when on-road. Typical pressures for off and on-road conditions are 40psi and 65psi respectively. If you do not possess a pressure gauge then squeeze the tyre sides. You should be able to press your thumb about 5mm into the side of the tyre. Inspect the tyre for adequacy of tread all around the circumference and for cuts in the

Above. On the forest tracks, Canaston Woods.

sidewall and replace if there are any shortcomings.

WHEEL TIGHTNESS CHECK

Many modern bikes now have their wheels secured by quick release levers. These are extremely convenient and effective, but it is important to ensure that they are correctly tightened, because failure to do so could be the cause of a very nasty accident. A correctly closed quick release lever will curve in toward the wheel when tightened and the annotation 'closed' should be seen on the lever. In principle it is a cam device and provided it is tightened with enough force to leave a slight imprint on your hand, it will not come open on its own.

After a ride ensure your bike is thoroughly cleaned, checked and lubricated. Any problems should be rectified by a competent mechanic. Doing this after a ride should ensure that you take action in time for your next outing. Cycle shops usually require a few days to complete repairs and it is unfair to turn up and expect the mechanic to fix a problem there and then.

MENDING A PUNCTURE ON A RIDE

The first observation to make here is that this will be a very unlikely occurrence as you will be carrying a spare tube (I often carry two). It is surprising how soon you can become chilled and your willpower starts to go if you stop to repair a puncture on a cold day. You will need to have with you:

- a puncture outfit
- tyre levers
- an adjustable spanner if you do not have quick release levers
- a pump

NB: If you are merely changing the tube, follow Instructions 1, 2, 3, 7, 10, 11 and 12.

1. Undo the wheel nuts. Release the brake cable if necessary, to enable the tyre to pass between the brake blocks.
2. Remove the tyre from the rim, only using levers if unavoidable — many mountain bike tyres can be removed without the use of levers and this is preferable to avoid the risk of pinching the tube and causing additional holes. If using levers insert them about 80mm apart and push them down together. Then insert the third lever and push it down. Remove the middle one and edge around the tyre until you can release the remaining amount of tyre by hand.
3. Remove the dust cap and valve securing nut and push the valve through the rim and then gently pull the tube out of the tyre.
4. Inflate the tube sufficiently to locate the puncture. Pass the tube close to your ear or lips to locate the escape of air. Mark the position of the puncture with a cross using the small crayon from the puncture repair outfit, or alternatively gently insert a small pin into the puncture.
5. Let the air out of the tyre and sandpaper the area vigorously to clean and roughen it. Select the minimum size patch necessary for the repair.
6. Spread a thin layer of glue over an area slightly larger than the proposed patch and allow to dry for 5min.
7. While waiting for the glue to dry, check

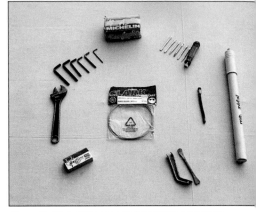

Above: Cycle maintenance and mending a puncture.

the tyre for the cause of the puncture and remove it. If you are unable to find a cause, check that the spokes are not protruding through the rim and rim tape. You should be able to use the distance of the puncture from the valve to guide you to the cause.
8. Remove the foil from the patch and apply to the tyre, pressing down firmly all over. Pinch the patch to split the backing paper and gently peel off — this minimises the chance of lifting the edge of the patch. Dust the area with some dusted chalk or talcum powder.
9. Inflate the tyre sufficiently for a test. Carefully check for further punctures — they often come in twos and threes — then deflate.
10. Place the tube inside the tyre and insert the valve through the hole in the rim. Inflate with a very low pressure to prevent 'pinching' of the tube. Ensure the tube is completely inside the tyre and then gently ease the tyre back inside the rim. Use the palms of your hands if possible to minimise the chance of a pinch, using the levers only if absolutely necessary. If using levers, double check that there is no chance of pinching the tube between lever and rim.
11. Fully reinflate the tyre with a pressure appropriate to road or off-road use. Replace the valve securing nut and dust cap. Check that the cover is positioned correctly by spinning the wheel, and deflate and reposition if necessary.
12. Place the wheel into the frame of the bike and secure the nuts tightly. Check that the wheel is correctly positioned by spinning it and adjusting if necessary. Reconnect the brake cable and test the brakes.

Escaping from our towns and cities to go walking is easy. We gather up our boots and rucksack, climb in our cars or on the bus and just go. Cycling requires a little more planning. Bikes need a rack for transport by car and you are not permitted to take them on the bus, so the whole idea needs more careful thought. We have to consider exactly how we are going to make our great escape from the pressures of city or town life to the tranquil pleasures of cycling in the country. The first means of escape is by the bike itself, but the chances of escaping from the town or city without dangerous exposure to heavy traffic is unlikely, until the National Cycle Network makes significant progress.

USE OF THE RAILWAY

Without doubt, the best way to travel to the start of a ride is by rail, letting 'the train take the strain'. There are four basic railway routes that survive in Wales. The line from Chester to Holyhead takes you across the north of the country from east to west; the Shrewsbury to Dovey Junction to Pwllheli line takes you across the middle of the country; and the Newport to Pembroke line takes you across the south. In addition, there is the beautifully scenic Heart of Wales line that connects Shrewsbury via 120 miles of green rolling hills and the Brecon Beacons to the South Wales coast at Swansea. For some of the rides in this book it is possible to have a linear cycle ride and to use a train to return to the start. The Valley Lines route between Cardiff and Merthyr Tydfil is especially useful for this as it runs parallel with the Taff Trail for a considerable length. However, the position with regard to cycles on trains is complicated, seems to change often and depends on where in Wales you wish to travel. Most trains have a fairly restricted space for cycles. Each line can be served by a variety of different train designs and operated by different companies (there are six operating in Wales). The number of cycles carried can range from two to six; booking may not be necessary, may be recommended, or may even be compulsory;

and there may or may not be a charge. If you are considering transporting your bikes by rail, the most reliable advice that can be given is to contact a railway information office as early as possible. Either contact the National Rail Enquiry Line (0345 484950) or contact the train operating companies' Customer Services:

- Central Trains (Tel: 0121 654 3833)
- Great Western (Tel: 01793 499458)
- North Western Trains (Tel: 0161 228 2141)
- Valley Lines (Tel: 01222 430460)
- Virgin Trains (Tel: 0121 654 7400)
- Wales and West (Tel: 01222 430090)

If you do decide to use the train, make sure that you are on the platform in good time and report to the guard as soon as possible. It is best to wait three-quarters of the way towards the back end of the platform to spot the guard's van or bike storage section as it passes. With luck you will be seen and the doors will be opened. Prepare to load and unload your cycles yourself and be willing to move quickly. It is wise to tie a label onto your machine stating your name and destination. You should be most careful on Sundays as it is track maintenance day and it is important to ensure that the train will be running both ways without interruption. If a section of track is under maintenance, then buses are used to transport passengers and these are not permitted to carry cycles.

TRANSPORT BY CAR

If, like many of us, you are not lucky enough to be close to a railway station, you have only one way to get to the start of these rides, and that is by a car. It is possible to take your bike inside the car, if you remove one or more wheels, but that probably limits the number of cycles to be taken to just one. There is really no alternative other than to consider a cycle rack. There are two basic ways of carrying a bike: a rear-mounted carrier, and by the use of the roof.

The rear-mounted carrier is probably the least expensive method, but you are generally limited to two bikes, sometimes three. The bikes mount sideways across the rear of the car, and the one big advantage is that you can see them during your journey. However, there is a tendency to make the car tail heavy, and you must ensure that your rear number plate is not covered or you will be committing an offence. There are also regulations restricting how much your 'payload' can protrude over your rear lights. That is not to say that these carriers are not a good idea, as they provide a cost-effective solution, but it is important that you check and consider these things before you part with your hard-earned cash.

The other alternative is to carry the bikes on the roof. You can strap them down with bungees on top of a roof rack, in which case they will quickly become scratched. The best but most expensive solution is to purchase roof bars and special cycle carriers that clamp to them. Without doubt, the best type of roof bar-mounted cycle carrier is the type that secures the wheels in a channel that runs the length of the bike, and also clamps the diagonal member of the frame. These clamps are lockable and enable you to lock your bikes to the car. I have used one of these on a small Rover 100 and have found the arrangement very satisfactory for carrying as many as four bikes. Most car manufacturers have roof bars and matching cycle carriers available as part of their accessory range. It is probable that buying equipment specifically matched to your car will generally provide the best, if not the cheapest solution, although versions for multi-application are widely available from car accessory shops. Having firmly supported the advantages of roof bar carriers, there is also one disadvantage to be noted as I found to my cost in the lovely county town of Taunton on an otherwise idyllic August day three years ago. It is very easy to forget momentarily that there are cycles on the roof when entering car parks with restricted headroom, and this I duly did. Not only are many multi-storey car parks equipped with horizontal bars seemingly designed to cause maximum damage to cycles on the roof, but so, ironically, are many of the car parks specifically provided for many of the rides in this book. You will need to be vigilant if you use a roof bar carrier.

Below: Transporting bikes by car.

The Kerry Ridgeway.

THE LLANGOLLEN CANAL
LLANGOLLEN TO
PONTCYSYLLTE AQUEDUCT

*'The charm of Llangollen, as, indeed of all
Wales, lies in its contrasts. For here, in the
valley and foothills, are ancient homesteads
slumbering beneath the shade of forest trees that
would do credit to regions that have nothing
else to boast of but their timber.' Highways and
Byways of North Wales by A. G. Bradley*

This route describes a ride along the
Llangollen Canal in an easterly direction from
Llangollen Wharf to Pontcysyllte Aqueduct
and back. It is a ride that is made memorable
by the superb views south across the Vale of
Llangollen. An alternative short ride (3¹/₂
miles return) is to go west to Horseshoe Weir
and back. This is where some of the waters
from the River Dee are captured and fed into
the canal. This small section is only navigable
by small horse-drawn boats used for short
pleasure trips and is therefore quieter. The
ride forms part of one of the three relatively
short stretches of this canal that are regarded
by British Waterways as being open to
cycling, and is part of the Llangollen to Irish
Bridge stretch. The other two are from
Wrenbury to Grindley Brook, and Colemere
Country Park to Ellesmere. You are required
to display a valid cycling permit on your cycle
at all times, obtainable from British
Waterways' Ellesmere Office
(Tel: 01691 622549).

BACKGROUND AND PLACES OF INTEREST

The Llangollen Canal
This canal has a somewhat unusual nature as
it was built with two purposes in mind. The
first was the normal one of transporting the
heavy goods of the time. Before canals, loads
were limited to the few hundred kilogrammes
that a pack horse or a horse-drawn wagon
could draw over the rutted roads of the time,
so the lower cost of transport led to a
significant spurt of economic development.
The second purpose of the Llangollen Canal
was to act as a supplier of water from the
River Dee. A large horseshoe-shaped weir,
designed by Thomas Telford, extracts water
from the river into the canal which is then fed
to a reservoir at Hurleston in Cheshire where
it is treated and used as drinking water. This

Below: Busy times at Llangollen Wharf.

Above: Pontcysyllte Aqueduct.

the River Dee. It is perhaps most famous for its annual International Musical Eisteddfod staged in July which has been held since 1947. The competitions include events for choirs, soloists, dancing and folk singing. Above Llangollen are the striking ruins of Castell Dinas Bran with its fang-like elements of crumbling masonry, standing at one of the very gates into Wales and dominating the vale below. Almost everyone has heard of the Ladies of Llangollen — two eccentric Irish women who secretly eloped from their homes in Ireland to devote their lives to 'Friendship, celibacy, and the knitting of blue stockings' at their home Plas Newydd. They were famous for their peculiarities of dress and their collection of curiosities and old oak, and it became the custom that their visitors, of whom there were many, should contribute to their collection. Among the famous visitors to their home were the Duke of Wellington, the Duke of Gloucester, William Wordsworth and Sir Walter Scott. Plas Newydd is open from Easter through to October (Tel: 01978 861314 for more information).

Llangollen Steam Railway

This is a steam and diesel heritage railway and represents some excellent enthusiasts' work which has brought the railway back to life since 1975. There are five stations open — some of which have either been restored or completely rebuilt — and about 5 miles of track between Llangollen and Carrog stations. Llangollen station is situated immediately by the bridge over the River Dee and is only a short distance from the town centre and the canal wharf. There are several trains per day throughout the year. (Tel: 01978 860951 for talking timetable, or 01978 860979 for general enquiries.)

additional purpose saved the canal from extinction when many others were abandoned in the mid-19th century when trains were introduced. At the end of the ride is Thomas Telford's magnificent Pontcysyllte Aqueduct. This was completed in 1805 and, supported by 18 piers, it carries the canal 121ft above the valley floor. There are some very enjoyable trips by boat available from Llangollen Wharf, including a 2hr journey over the aqueduct to Froncysyllte, or horse-drawn trips to Horseshoe Weir.
(Tel: 01691 690322).

Llangollen

This small town, although rather a traffic bottleneck in summer, is picturesquely set among wooded hills and lies mainly on the south bank of

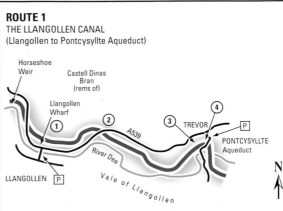

ROUTE 1
THE LLANGOLLEN CANAL
(Llangollen to Pontcysyllte Aqueduct)

Left: Berwyn station on the Llangollen Steam Railway.

Starting Point: Llangollen Wharf — look for prominent brown signs.

Parking and Toilets: At the free visitors' car park close to the BBC Doctor Who Exhibition. There is also parking available at the end of the ride close to the Pontcysyllte Aqueduct at Trevor Wharf.

Distance: 4.2 miles (8.4 miles there and back).

Maps: Ordnance Survey Landranger Sheet 117.

Hills: None.

Surface: The towpath alternates between a gravel base and a grassy surface.

Safety: Care should be taken when cycling under the canal bridges as their curved nature could lead to a nasty blow on the head or shoulder. Also, some parts of the towpath are rutted in places and the grassed parts are likely to be greasy in wet weather. Cycling is not allowed across the Pontcysyllte Aqueduct. If you cycle to Horseshoe Weir, take care when passing the towing horses.

Roads and Road Crossings: At the end of the ride it is necessary to cycle on a quiet stretch of road at Trevor to cross the canal spur and regain the towpath by the Pontcysyllte Aqueduct.

Refreshments: A large choice in Llangollen. There is also the Telford Inn at the end of the ride at Trevor.

Nearest Tourist Information Centre: Town Hall, Castle Street, Llangollen LL20 5PD (Tel: 01978 860828).

ROUTE INSTRUCTIONS
As some of the towpath is a grassy surface it is more appropriate to undertake this ride in dry conditions.

1. (0 miles): From Llangollen Wharf commence cycling east.

2. (1.7 miles): There are outstanding views south across the Vale of Llangollen to the hills beyond.

3. (4.1 miles): The towpath is obstructed here and you have to change to the other side of the canal, by using the steel and wood bridge.

4. (4.2 miles): When you meet the small road, you need to cross the canal spur at Trevor Wharf. Turn left and proceed for 200yd or so and turn right into New Road and over the 'Weak Bridge' at Pontwan. Turn right into the brick-paved approach to the car park and this takes you to the east side of the canal where you can walk across the Pontcysyllte Aqueduct or enjoy a 45min boat trip. (Cycling is not permitted across the aqueduct.)

RHYL TO PRESTATYN
A SEA WALL RIDE

'I like windy Rhyl. The tide was far out and the gold sands stretched for miles. It is one of the many seaside places in Great Britain which have grown up almost within modern times to satisfy the migratory instincts of great industrial cities.' H. V. Morton from *In Search of Wales*

I owe the discovery of this short ride to a chance encounter with a very knowledgeable cyclist that I met a few days earlier on the Lôn Eifion Cycleway. You will not find mention of it in any cycling publications that I know of, but it is a unique ride that takes place on a mixture of promenade and sea wall. If the weather is similar to the weather that I experienced, you will probably find that the wind will virtually blow you from Rhyl to Prestatyn, so it will not be until the return leg that you will receive your beneficial exercise. If you are taking a seaside holiday in Rhyl or Prestatyn and the children have spent all your money, then take a day off and refresh yourselves, enjoy the sea air and perhaps find a nice quiet secluded beach away from everyone else.

BACKGROUND AND PLACES OF INTEREST

Rhyl and Prestatyn

Rhyl and Prestatyn are holiday resorts that are to all intents and purposes linked together. They have little past to speak of but

boast the freshest air in Wales. In local Rhyl literature there is the story of the town being so healthy that the citizens were compelled to shoot a man to start the local cemetery. The beaches are extensive and splendid and these resorts cater very well for families who want a seaside holiday. Prestatyn is at the north end of Offa's Dyke. The main area catering for the holidaymaker is Central Beach. Here there are many attractions, including the Nova Centre which is open the whole year round (Tel: 01745 888021) and includes a pool and fitness facilities and an Offa's Dyke Centre. Rhyl lies on the east side of the River Clwyd and has a parade of over 2 miles long. The attractions here are the Sky Tower, open daily from Easter to October (Tel: 01745 331071) and a Sea Life Centre, again open daily (Tel: 01745 344660). The Sun Centre provides swimming and water entertainment (Tel: 01745 344433).

St Asaph

St Asaph is built on a rise between the Elwy and Clwyd rivers and has been a centre of religion since Asaph founded his movement here in the 6th century. It is a very small place, but due to its cathedral is classified as a city. The cathedral is the smallest medieval example in Britain. Today's building was originally constructed in the 13th century but was burnt in 1402 and restored afterwards. The tower was destroyed in a storm and rebuilt in 1715. Further restoration work was carried out in 1869-75 and 1929-32. There is a cathedral museum containing early bibles and prayer books that can be viewed on request.

Left: The Sea Life Centre in Rhyl.

Starting Point: From the Sea Life Centre in Rhyl.

Parking and Toilets: There are plenty of car parks in Rhyl, just drive along East Parade and find one reasonably close to the Sea Life Centre.

Distance: 4.1 miles (8.2 miles there and back).

Maps: Ordnance Survey Landranger Sheet 116.

Hills: Absolutely none.

Surface: Usually the concrete sea wall or paved promenade.

Safety: There are no safety hazards on this ride.

Roads and Road Crossings: None.

Refreshments: There is a Pontins Hotel at the end of Marine Drive in Prestatyn.

Nearest Tourist Information Centre: Rhyl Children's Village, West Parade, Rhyl LL18 1HZ (Tel: 01745 355068).

Cycle Hire: Happy Hire, The Pier, Colwyn Bay (Tel: 01352 758984).

Right: Amusements at Rhyl.

Below: Towards Prestatyn on the sea wall.

ROUTE INSTRUCTIONS

Basically no instructions are necessary for this ride. Just cycle from the Sea Life Centre in Rhyl eastwards to Prestatyn (Barkby Beach). The ride takes place initially on Rhyl Promenade and then on sea defences which usually slope gently towards the sea. After you leave the amusements of Rhyl, you are accompanied by bungalow suburbia for a while and then by Rhyl Golf Links. After that there is the splendid Ffrith Beach and then back to further seaside amusements, this time belonging to Prestatyn. The ride ends at Barkby Beach Pitch and Putt Golf Course.

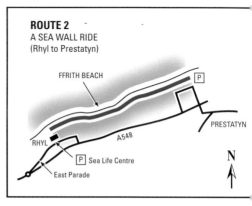

LLYN BRENIG
A CIRCULAR RIDE AROUND THE RESERVOIR FROM THE VISITOR CENTRE

'The western wall of the Vale is not so sharply marked. The slope towards the Hiraethog is much more gradual, valley rising above valley, ridge above ridge.' A. G. Bradley, describing the area around Llyn Brenig from his *Highways and Byways in North Wales*

This is a mostly flat but nicely varied ride with lots of interest, and it provided us with a most enjoyable and relaxing day. Buzzards with their plaintiff cries invariably wheeled overhead; aircraft from a nearby fighter base practised some exciting flying over the reservoir; and scores of fly fishermen practised their art from ashore and afloat. The first part of the ride through extensive woodland of Sitka spruce is on a quiet tarmac road that is virtually traffic-free and runs along the western side of the reservoir. This is followed by a short section of just over 2 miles along a B road that is fast but wide and not very busy. The section along the eastern side of the reservoir is completely traffic-free and is along a stone-based track. The final leg of the ride is again traffic-free and runs along the top of the reservoir dam.

BACKGROUND AND PLACES OF INTEREST

Llyn Brenig Reservoir
The reservoir was completed in 1976 and was opened by HRH The Prince of Wales. Its main function, in conjunction with Lake Bala and Llyn Celyn, is to regulate the flow of the River Dee and provide water for the houses and industry of North East Wales. It covers an area of 920 acres and lies in an attractive setting high up in the heart of the Denbigh Moors. On the east side of the lake is an archaeological trail of 2 miles with remains from the Bronze Age and of 16th century farmhouses. It is a leading centre for fly fishing, sailing and bird watching. The visitor centre has an interesting exhibition moving through time from primeval seas through to a modern river regulating dam, and also a lakeside café and gift shop. There is a fleet of 10 mountain bikes for hire. The centre is open for seven days a week in the summer and in the winter by arrangement (Tel: 01490 420463 for more information).

Left: The fly fishermen of Llyn Brenig.

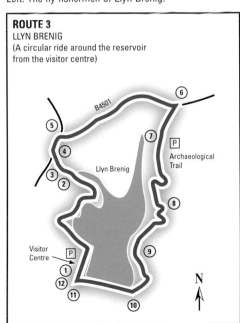

ROUTE 3
LLYN BRENIG
(A circular ride around the reservoir from the visitor centre)

Denbigh and the Vale of Clwyd

Denbigh is a pleasant country town, but most people visit Denbigh for its castle which is situated on a hill overlooking the Vale of Clwyd which lies to the east. When you have finished climbing up the long steep street to the market place, there is a further climb if you are to enjoy the full beauties of the place and see the castle. It is laid out as an irregular pentagon and to a large extent lies in ruins, with the exception of its impressive gatehouse. The archway that spans the entrance bears a badly disfigured statue which is probably Edward I or Henry de Lacy, Earl of Lincoln. The tower of St Hilary's Church lies to the north of the chapel entrance which is all that remains of the chapel demolished in 1923.

Clocaenog Forest

Situated on Mynydd Hiraethog, the Forestry Commission has tried hard to ease the desolation of the area and cover the earth with a great dome of trees called Clocaenog Forest. It is criss-crossed by several roads which have attractive picnic spots, one of the best being at Pont Petryal where there is a tree-fringed pool. The Forestry Commission claims that this is red squirrel country. There is a visitor centre at Bod Petrual in an old gamekeeper's cottage and this tells the story of the forest. (Open daily 10.00-17.00 from Easter to September.)

Below: Remains of the stone circle by Llyn Brenig.

Above: View from the ramparts of Denbigh castle.
Welsh Tourist Board

Starting Point: Llyn Brenig Reservoir Visitor Centre. This is situated just off the B4501 about 6 miles north of Cerrigydrudion.

Parking and Toilets: Park in the visitor centre car park, or the Archaeological Trail car park which is about half-way round the ride. There are toilets at both places.

Distance: 9.6 miles round trip.

Maps: Ordnance Survey Landranger Sheet 116.

Hills: There is only one significant hill which is about half-way round, on the B4501.

Surface: Generally good and well drained, a mixture of tarmac and stone-based track.

Safety: Care should be taken on the B4501 which tends to be a fast road.

Roads and Road Crossings: Approximately 2 miles of this ride are on quiet forestry roads in the Llyn Brenig woodland area where only the occasional vehicle is encountered. About a further 2 miles are on a 'B' classification road. The remainder of the road — a little under 4 miles — is completely traffic-free.

Refreshments: Refreshments are available at the visitor centre.

Nearest Tourist Information Centre: Royal Oak Stables, Betws-y-coed LL24 0AH (Tel: 01690 710426).

Cycle Hire: There are cycles available for hire for either 2hr or for one day from the visitor centre.

ROUTE INSTRUCTIONS

1. (0 miles): From the top of the car park, turn right onto the quiet road to travel north and when you are at the sailing club take a sharp turn left. You basically follow the western shore of the reservoir.

2. (2.0 miles): Instead of following the road around to the right, take the lesser road which effectively takes you straight on and which is signposted 'Nature Trail'.

3. (2.5 miles): By the five-bar wooden gate, carry straight on along the lesser-used pot-holed track.

4. (2.6 miles): At the cattle grid and five-bar wooden gate you will meet the B4501. Turn right here, which is a fast road, so be careful.

5. (2.9 miles): Turn right to continue on the B4501 — signposted 'Nantglyn 7'.

6. (4.8 miles): Turn right from the B4501 and take the minor road (signposted to Archaeological Trail Car Park, Bird Hide and Toilets).

7. (5.5 miles): At the car park, bear left through the six-bar wooden gate to the left of the toilet block.

8. (6.7 miles): Pass through one of a pair of gates to enter a more wooded section.

9. (7.9 miles): Pass through a further gate.

10. (8.5 miles): Turn right to traverse along the dam.

11. (9.3 miles): Leave the dam by turning right, taking the track back to the visitor centre.

12. (9.6 miles): Arrive back at the car park.

GWYDYR FOREST PARK
A CIRCULAR CYCLE TRAIL AROUND THE FOREST

'Gwydir lieth two bowshots above the river Conwy; it is a pretty place.' Leland, writing in 1536

Gwydyr Forest Park consists of over 7,000 acres of woodland that is run by Forest Enterprise and includes mountain streams, waterfalls and lakes. The area includes the well-known Swallow Falls and the tourist village of Betws-y-coed. Two mountain bike routes are laid out in the forest park, one of $10^1/_2$ miles on the north side of the A5(T) and one of $6^1/_2$ miles on the south side. It is the longer one that is the subject of this ride. The routes are exceptionally well waymarked and it is difficult to go wrong. The first part of the ride is on a very quiet country road and this is followed unfortunately with a long steep section of about $1^1/_2$ miles as you climb up to Llyn y Parc, making this a demanding ride. Most of the ride is on gravelled forest paths with only the occasional short section on a quiet country road. Forest Enterprise produces an excellent full-colour leaflet with detailed mapping and this is available for a small charge from the nearby Betws-y-coed Tourist Information Centre. It provides details of the rides and of various walking trails. The leaflet also doubles as a cycle permit.

BACKGROUND AND PLACES OF INTEREST

Gwydyr Forest Park and the Mining Activities
The forest extends across the hills on the edge of Snowdonia. The flat pasture land of the Conwy Valley suddenly rises steeply to the wooded hills above. The forest is easily accessible due to many tracks, old miners' paths, well-established forest footpaths and, I am pleased to say, cycle trails. There are many parking and picnic sites and no less than nine well-waymarked walks. The Forestry Commission began replanting in 1921 to replace the heavy felling that took place during World War 1. An attractive range of broadleaved trees were planted on the lower slopes as well as silver fir and Douglas fir. These are now reaching an elegant maturity and are being felled and replanted. On the higher areas, pines and spruces were planted. There are extensive mineral workings in the forest park area. The mineral potential of the area was first developed as early as the first part of the 17th century. Mining for minerals was the main industry of the area for three centuries. Lead and zinc were the main materials and this work reached a peak between 1850 and 1919. Hidden in the forest you will find old engine-houses, waste tips and reservoirs and several of the larger mines have been made safe for people to visit.

Below: The waymarking is superb in Gwydyr Forest.

Above: Llyn y Parc.

Gwydir Castle

Gwydir Castle is an Elizabethan house with gardens but its history goes back still further. It is situated in the Vale of Conwy beneath Carreg y Gwalch. The Wynn family, descended from the kings of Gwynedd, were one of the most prestigious families in North Wales during the Tudor and Stuart periods and this is their ancestral home. It is said that Dafydd ap Siencyin, the Welsh version of Robin Hood, haunts the castle. In fact, the castle is reportedly one of the most haunted houses in Wales. Although the building is mainly 16th and 19th century around a 14th century hall, there was a fortification here as far back as the seventh century. Recently the castle has been going through a period of restoration and conservation but it is still open to the public every day from 10am to 5pm. The gardens are known for their peacocks and they include glorious cedar trees which were planted to celebrate the wedding of Charles I.

Betws-y-coed

Come rain or shine, Betws-y-coed is always popular with tourists. The meaning of its name, 'the oratory in the forest', illustrates its unique charm and beauty. Although the main street along the A5 is very busy, lined with hotels, cafés and shops, you can soon escape the bustle of the village and take numerous, beautiful walks along the River Llugwy to Swallow Falls, through the glorious Gwydyr Forest, up through oaks and beeches to the islanded lake of Elsi or southward to the Fairy Glen and fine falls on the Conwy and Machno rivers. There are several bridges of note in and around the village: the iron Waterloo Bridge (1815), the 17th-century stone bridge of Pont-y-pair (over the Llugwy), Pont-ar-Lledr (over the Lledr) and Pont-yr-afanc (over the Conwy). If the weather is inclement then why not visit either the railway museum or the motor museum or browse through some of the many craft shops catering for all tastes, from pottery and jewellery to ethnic goods from Africa!

Starting Point: From the pay-and-display car park near the junction of the A5(T) and the B5106 road to Llanrwst and Gwydir Castle.

Parking and Toilets: The car park at the starting point (above) has toilets. There are a couple of additional parking possibilities at Llyn Geirionydd and Ty'n Llwyn.

Distance: 10 miles round trip.

Maps: Ordnance Survey Landranger Sheet 115.

Hills: There is a significant climb at the beginning of the ride for about 1¹/₂ miles.

Surface: Most of this ride is on gravelled forest tracks and most of the surface is very good.

Safety: Although this is an easy ride from a mountain biking viewpoint, it needs to be treated with respect by the novice. The advice of Forest Enterprise is that the route is not suitable for children under 10 years of age. A mountain bike and a cycle helmet are essential for this ride.

Roads and Road Crossings: A small amount of this ride (about 2½ miles) is

Below: The long steep section up to Llyn y Parc.

on quiet country lanes, but no busy roads are crossed.

Refreshments: There are no refreshments actually on the ride — Betws-y-coed is the nearest place for refreshments. We took a picnic and enjoyed it by Llyn y Parc.

Nearest Tourist Information Centre: Royal Oak Stables, Betws-y-coed LL24 0AH.

Cycle Hire: Mountain bikes can be hired from Beics Betws, behind the Tan Lan Restaurant in Betws-y-coed.

ROUTE INSTRUCTIONS
This circular route is extremely well waymarked. Just follow the green bicycle logo; no directions are necessary.

ROUTE 4
GWYDYR FOREST PARK
(A circular cycle trail around the forest

Hafna Mine (dis)

P   Llyn y Parc

Llyn Goddionduon

Llyn y Sarnau

Cyffty Mine (dis)

P

TY'N LLWYN

B5106 to Gwydyr Castle

P

A5(T)

N

BETWS-Y-COED

THE MINERS' TRACK
A SHORT AND SURPRISINGLY EASY RIDE ON THE LOWER SLOPES OF SNOWDON FROM PEN-Y-PASS

'Easy to say, "Behold Eryri",
But difficult to reach its head;
Easy for him whose hopes are cheery
To bid the wretch be comforted.'
Welsh proverb

George Borrow — the Victorian travel writer — climbed Snowdon in 1854, arm in arm with his daughter singing this Welsh stanza at the top of his voice. He did not take this easy route starting from Pen-y-Pass, already at an altitude of 1,100ft at the top of the Llanberis Pass, but instead started from Llanberis itself. The Miners' Track takes you past the small Llyn Teyrn, and then across a causeway at one end of Llyn Llydaw that was constructed in 1853 to make it easier to transport copper from the mines to Pen-y-Pass. From this causeway there is a magnificent panorama of the whole of the Snowdon Horseshoe. Alongside Llyn Llydaw you can see many of the remains of the buildings that were associated with the Britannia Copper Mine, including the ore-crushing mill and the miners' barracks. The situation was so remote that the miners lived here during the week, to return on foot over the Glyder Mountains to their homes at Bethesda at weekends. It must have been a desperate existence living up here in the winter, although on the rare occasions of a sunny day in the summer, living alongside Llyn Llydaw must have had its attractions. The Miners' Track is a bridleway and therefore cycleable as far as the ore-crushing mill. After this it becomes a footpath and therefore cannot be legally cycled. It is, in fact, one of the easier ways to ascend Snowdon, but ascending Snowdon on a bike is, in my view, an extreme sport and we will stick to the (almost) flat part. It should be noted that the Snowdonia voluntary cycling agreement applies on this bridleway. This means that between 1 June and 30 September there is no cycling on Snowdon bridleways between 10am and 5pm. Outside of this there is no restriction.

Below: The scattered town of Llanberis.
Welsh Tourist Board.

BACKGROUND AND PLACES OF INTEREST

Snowdon

Snowdon, or Eryri to give it its Welsh name, is the term for the mountainous region of the area and not a single mountain. The English name is thought to have been bestowed originally by the Saxons who named it the Snow Dun — the Snow Hill or fortress — due to it being so imposing and snow-covered for many months of the year. Eryri in Welsh seems to mean either a breeding place of eagles or a rugged excrescence. The name for the highest peak — that most people call Snowdon — is Yr Wyddfa Fawr (The Great Tomb). A glance at the map of the area tells us something of the myths and legends of these mountains — the names of the geological features are poetic — Yr Elen (Hill of the Fawn); Castell y Gwynt (Castle of the Winds); Ffynnon Lloer (Well of the Moon); Pen yr Ole Wen (Hill of the White Light). Snowdon is the highest mountain south of Scotland and is 3,560ft high. The surrounding area is perhaps unsurpassed for rugged beauty which was described by George Borrow as only he could: 'Perhaps in the whole world there is no more picturesquely beautiful region than Snowdon, a region of mountains, lakes, cataracts and groves, in which Nature shows herself in her most grand and beautiful forms.' Welsh legend variously connects King Arthur with these parts and he fought his last battle at Bwlch-y-Saethau (Pass of Arrows), after which the Knights of the Round Table retreated to a

cave to wait in slumber for their king to rise again. Llyn Llydaw is often thought to be the lake where Excalibur was thrown.

Llanberis

Llanberis is a scattered town at the foot of Snowdon, and there are many very interesting attractions here of which there is only space to mention a few. As a starter you can ascend Snowdon on the Snowdon Mountain Railway. This is a wonderful feat of Victorian engineering. It was opened in 1896 and is the only rack-and-pinion line in Britain. It is operated by a fleet of seven steam locomotives, some dating from 1895, and four diesels. It takes about an hour to reach the summit and the train waits there for about half an hour before the return journey which takes a further hour. Trains do not run to a strict timetable; the capacity of each train is 59 passengers but there has to be a minimum of 25. Operation is also dependent upon the weather, so you would do well to arrive at the station early. The railway is open from mid-March until October (Tel: 01286 870223 for more information). As you might expect from the land of narrow gauge steam railways there is a further railway attraction in Llanberis. This is the Llanberis Lake Railway which was the original quarry railway to Port Dinorwic on the Menai Strait. At first it was worked by animal power and gravity but it later became a 4ft gauge railway operated by steam power. It was saved by enthusiasts and is now narrow gauge but is still steam. (Tel: 01286 870549). The Welsh Slate Museum is at the former Dinorwig Quarry which was in operation from 1809 to 1969 and in 1900 employed as many as 3,000 people. A large amount of the original machinery is still there and the wheel is one of the largest in Britain at over 50ft in diameter. (Tel: 01286 870630 for more information.)

Pen-y-Pass

Pen-y-Pass is at the head of the Llanberis Pass which is one of the most desolate and forlorn valleys in Wales, with towering rocks above you and huge boulders on either side. Pen-y-Pass is the starting place for the ride and here there is a youth hostel, mountain rescue centre and café. There are lots of old photographs reproduced on the walls of the café giving a flavour of walking expeditions in Victorian times.

ROUTE 5
THE MINERS' TRACK
(A short and surprisingly easy ride up the lower slopes of Snowdon from Pen-y-Pass)

A4086
PEN-Y-PASS
1
P
2
Miners' Track
Llyn Teyrn
3
Llyn Llydaw
N

Starting Point: From the car park at Pen-y-Pass.

Parking and Toilets: Park in the car park at Pen-y-Pass where there is a full range of facilities.

Distance: 2.1 miles (4.2 miles there and back).

Maps: Ordnance Survey Landranger Sheet 115.

Hills: The outward leg is a steady climb almost all of the way.

Surface: The Miners' Track is a bridleway and is a comparatively rough surface of bedded-down stones for most of its length with diagonally situated drainage channels at regular intervals, so you need to be fairly careful about where you place your wheel.

Safety: The comparatively rough surface necessitates the use of a mountain bike. In places there is a considerable drop near the edge of the track, so I would advise that this route is not suitable for children under 10 years of age. As you are considerably over 300m above sea level here, the weather can change quickly, so make sure you have a good idea what the weather is going to do and take appropriate clothing.

Below: Panoramic view of the slopes of Snowdon with the railway running along the ridge. *Welsh Tourist Board*

Right: The Snowdon Mountain Railway at the start of the route.

Roads and Road Crossings: None.

Refreshments: There is a comfortable café at the visitor centre at Pen-y-Pass. If you are lucky enough to experience a fine day then my suggestion would be to take a packed lunch and stop at the end of the ride alongside Llyn Llydaw.

Nearest Tourist Information Centre: 41a High Street, Llanberis LL55 4EU.

Cycle Hire: Beics Eryri, Caernarfon (Tel: 01286 676637).

ROUTE INSTRUCTIONS

Very few instructions are required for this ride. Basically you follow the bridleway up to the old copper mine buildings at Llyn Llydaw reservoir.

1. (0 miles): From the car park pass through the wooden five-bar gate and start the route which is initially quite steep.

2. (0.8 miles): Bear right, away from the track leading you to Llyn Teyrn to keep to The Miners' Track that will take you to the causeway across Llyn Llydaw.

3. (2.1 miles): Arrive at the derelict ore-crushing mill by the side of Llyn Llydaw.

LÔN LAS OGWEN
PORTH PENRHYN TO GLASINFRYN

'Bangor with an early morning sun over it is one of the freshest and most stimulating cities you can imagine.' H. V. Morton from *In Search of Wales*

This ride is another example of a route following the line of an old narrow gauge railway. This one was originally built by the Penrhyn Estate to transport slate from quarries at Bethesda to Porth Penrhyn (near Bangor) for onward shipping. The section from Porth Penrhyn follows the small River Cegin and this part is also known as Lôn Bach. The path was created by volunteer action in the 1980s and was subsequently upgraded and extended by Arfon Borough Council. It is a permissive path and provides a valuable opportunity for the cyclist to enjoy a riverine and woodland environment of considerable diversity. Although you pass through urban areas at first, you are largely unaware of this as you are screened from civilisation by the shaded woodlands of the Cegin Valley. It is a small oasis of nature that has survived thanks to the topography of the land and Gwynedd Council. Further south, by the A5, you can admire the skill of the engineers who built the main line railway — for example the viaduct at Glasinfryn, now not used but still there for all to admire. Gwynedd Council hope eventually to extend the path further to Bethesda, and this will provide a wonderful traffic-free opportunity to cycle to the splendid Carneddau mountains and the very heart of north Gwynedd.

BACKGROUND AND PLACES OF INTEREST

History of the Railway Line
The Penrhyn quarries that produced the slate in Bethesda were started in 1770 by Richard Pennant, the 1st Baron Penrhyn, and was the biggest opencast system in the world, forming a vast amphitheatre 1 mile long and 1,200ft deep. The quarry works railway that the route follows was constructed between 1870 and 1879. Before this the slate from Bethesda was transported by pack horse, or mules and carts, and by a tramroad

Below: There are fine views from the line.

constructed in 1801. Pont Marchogion is an 18th century masonry bridge which can be seen near Porth Penrhyn and once formed part of that tramroad. The inevitable decline of the slate industry in recent years and significant road system improvements led to the closure of the line in 1962.

Bangor

Bangor has a population of around 12,000 and is noted mainly for its cathedral and the University College of North Wales. Significant change came in the 19th century due to the increased commercial activity in the area. The Penrhyn Quarries in Bethesda, the development of Porth Penrhyn and the arrival of Telford's magnificent road (the current A5) and his Menai Suspension Bridge were notable developments. A little later, in 1848, the railway arrived and just two years later Stephenson's tubular bridge was completed. Places to visit include the old pier of 1896 which reaches halfway across the Menai Strait and which has now been restored to its original Victorian splendour. There is also the Museum of Welsh Antiquities and Art Gallery which has prehistoric and Roman material, 18th and 19th century furniture and costume, and is open Tuesdays to Saturdays. (Tel: 01248 353368 for more information.)

Anglesey and the Menai Strait

Anglesey's name is thought to derive from the Island of the Angles or possibly from the Norse 'ongull' meaning fiord or strait. It is scenically unspectacular but has some pleasant cliffs on Holy Island. The Menai Strait is about 13 miles long and varies between 200yd and 1 mile wide. Near Bangor the strait is crossed by two famous bridges — the Menai Suspension Bridge built by Thomas Telford in 1819-26, and the Britannia Bridge which was originally a tubular railway bridge built by Robert Stephenson but was destroyed by fire in 1970. A new bridge was built in 1972 with an additional deck added for the A5 road. Before these bridges, crossings were made by ferry but cattle were forced to swim.

Below: Lôn Bach — a well-signposted route.

ROUTE 6
LÔN LAS OGWFN
(Porth Penrhyn to Glasinfryn)

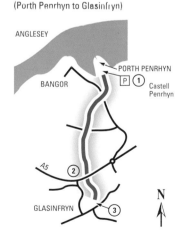

ANGLESEY

PORTH PENRHYN

BANGOR

Castell Penrhyn

A5

GLASINFRYN

N

Starting Point: The ride starts from Porth Penrhyn, near Bangor.

Parking and Toilets: Park in the car park by the Porth Penrhyn Dockmaster Office.

Distance: 3.0 miles (6.0 miles there and back), although this may be extended in the near future.

Maps: Ordnance Survey Landranger Sheet 115.

Hills: There are no significant hills on this ride.

Surface: Very good — mostly a gravelled surface.

Safety: There are no significant hazards on this ride. Care should be taken on the road when you pass under the A5.

Roads and Road Crossings: Just one very short section of road as you pass under the A5.

Refreshments: Definitely a 'take your own picnic ride', as I did not detect any possibility of purchasing refreshments on the way. Plan to enjoy the views of the distant Carneddau and Glyder mountain ranges while you picnic.

Nearest Tourist Information Centre: Town Hall, Deiniol Road, Bangor LL57 2RE.

Above: The start of the ride at Porth Penrhyn.

Cycle Hire: Snowdonia Mountain Biking, Bangor (Tel: 01248 353789).
West End Cycles, Bangor (Tel: 01248 371158).

ROUTE INSTRUCTIONS
Few instructions are necessary as this is a waymarked cycle path.

1. (0 miles): The ride starts by passing under the small arched bridge, and after a couple of hundred yards you pass over a wooden bridge.

2. (2.4 miles): The cycle path ends at a road. Take this to pass under the A5 and then turn left through the wooden gate to travel across an old red sandstone viaduct. Alternatively, if you wish to proceed into the pretty village of Glasinfryn, keep on the road and avoid the left turn through the gate.

3. (3.0 miles): The route currently ends when you meet the B4366 by Railway Cottages. However, there are plans to extend the route on toward Bethesda in the near future and some of this work may well have taken place by the time that this book appears in print.

LÔN LAS MENAI
CAERNARFON TO Y FELINHELI

'In the Welsh language it has always been called "Mon Mam Cym", which means "Mona the Mother of Wales". When crops have failed in all other regions, this island, from the richness of its soil and its abundant produce, has been able to supply all Wales.'
Giraldus Cambrensis c1146-1223, writing about Anglesey

This excellent, almost completely traffic-free ride provides panoramic views of the turbulent waters and golden sands of the Menai Strait, and beyond, the green and productive fields of the Isle of Anglesey. In a similar way to Lôn Eifion, Lôn Las Menai forms an important leg of Lôn Las Cymru which is Route 8 of the National Cycle Network. The route is built on the former trackbed of the Bangor to Caernarfon Railway. It is a mainly compacted dust path that runs from Caernarfon parallel with the Menai Strait, through to the edge of the sheltered village of Y Felinheli, which was at one time a busy port. We had a breezy but wonderful morning cycling this route. We

were accompanied by herring gulls wheeling and swooping in the wind and large yachts being blown along the strait at great speed. Further information on this route can be obtained from the 'Gwynedd Recreational Routes' leaflet, published by Gwynedd Council and available from Tourist Information Offices. I have described the route as far as Y Felinheli but if you follow the route through the village using Beach Road and the High Street, it is possible to rejoin the path by the old station and continue a little further.

BACKGROUND AND PLACES OF INTEREST

Y Felinheli
This attractive village, also known as Port Dinorwic, was once a busy port that exported slate conveyed here from the quarries at Dinorwic. Most of the nautical activity now seems to be associated with the sailing of

Below: Plenty of interest along the way.

yachts. The village has its place in history as it was the crossing place for the Roman invasion of Anglesey, and was also regularly used by Vikings who sheltered here from weather and tides. There are very good views across the Menai Strait.

The Greenwood Centre

This is an innovative and imaginative attraction that provides 17 acres of beautiful woodland and meadowland to explore with many features. The centrepiece is a magnificently constructed medieval-style hall that was built in the 1990s and is probably the first of its kind to be constructed in North Wales for around 400 years. The design replicates the great halls of the Middle Ages that were constructed as dwellings by landowners and princes, and took six months to build. It is constructed from 40 tons of green oak and is held together by 500 large wooden pegs, with all the timber sanded and treated with linseed oil. The nine frames that form the main structure of the building reproduce various styles in use during medieval times. The centre is entirely devoted to wood and the many uses to which it is put, not only at home but in other civilisations. You can walk through a giant redwood tree, find out how oak has been used in Wales, learn about the Celtic tree calendar and enjoy many other interesting features. The centre is

Above: The Menai Strait.

Opposite page: The Garddfon Inn.

open daily from mid-March until the end of October. (Tel: 01248 671493 for more information.)

Beaumaris, Anglesey

The main attraction in nearby Beaumaris is yet another castle. It is a great unfinished masterpiece. Commenced in 1295 as the last of the massive Edwardian fortresses of the 13th century to be built in North Wales, funding ran out before the fortifications reached their planned height, although the castle was declared to be in a state of defence in 1298. The military architect was the brilliant James of St George who brought all of his experience to this construction on the *beau marais* (beautiful marsh) alongside the Menai Strait. From the military architecture viewpoint, it is the most technically perfect castle in the British Isles. To take the castle, there were four successive lines of fortifications and 14 major obstacles to overcome, in addition to hundreds of arrow slits and also a number of murder holes used to defend entrances. Beaumaris is otherwise a pleasant resort and important yachting centre with good views across the sands to the mountains beyond.

Starting Point: From the recommended car park at Tan y Bont or the castle. Alternatively, the ride can be started from the Victoria Dock car park.

Parking and Toilets: There are several car parks in Caernarfon and you will probably park in the vicinity of the castle. We parked in the Tan y Bont car park by the outer wall of the castle. National Cycle Route 8 runs right past this car park so it is easy to find your way to the start of the ride. Without doubt the most convenient car park is the one by Victoria Dock which is right by the start of Lôn Las Menai.

Distance: 4.6 miles (9.2 miles there and back).

Maps: Ordnance Survey Landranger Sheet 115.

Hills: Only one — a short steep climb out of Y Felinheli on the return leg.

Surface: The surface is very good and is mostly of the compacted dust type.

Safety: No special safety hazards. Care should be taken where the cycleway negotiates the A487(T) roundabout near the Plas Menai National Outdoor Pursuit Centre.

Roads and Road Crossings: There is a little road work in Y Felinheli if you want to travel from the cycleway to the waterside. There is also one fairly busy roundabout to negotiate, near the Plas Menai National Outdoor Pursuit Centre, where it is probably best to dismount for a short distance and use the pavement if you have young children.

Refreshments: There is a good-looking inn by the waterside in Y Felinheli, but no opportunities for refreshment en route.

Nearest Tourist Information Centre: Oriel Pendeitsh, Castle Street, Caernarfon LL55 2NA.

Cycle Hire: Cycle Hire, 1 Slate Quay, Caernarfon LL55 2PB (Tel: 01286 676804).

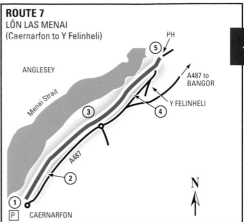

Beics Castell, 33 High Street, Caernarfon LL55 1RH (Tel: 01286 677400). Don's Bikes, 47 Pool Street, Caernarfon (Tel: 01286 677727).

ROUTE INSTRUCTIONS
Little instructions are necessary as the route is an obvious one.

1. (0 miles): Assuming that you have parked in the Tan y Bont car park, turn right to follow the Cycle Route 8 sign and follow the outer castle wall. Turn right by a block of apartments known as Glan-y-Mor, cycle straight on at the mini-roundabout and when you are close to the Victoria Dock car park pass through the barrier and pick up the cycle path that runs along the sea wall.

2. (1.0 miles): Be careful not to cycle down the lane serving the houses — this is not the cycle path — but find the cycle path on the right of the lane.

3. (2.6 miles): At the roundabout, walk your cycle straight over using the pavement and take the road marked 'Y Felinheli 1½', which is also marked by a blue Bangor cycle route sign. After a few yards, by the bus stop, the cycle route starts up again, initially running close to and parallel with the road, but eventually becoming screened by trees from the road.

4. (4.1 miles): At the end of the traffic-free cycleway, turn left onto Beach Road and cycle until you come to the old waterside area and inn.

5. (4.6 miles): Arrive at the waterside in Y Felinheli.

LÔN EIFION
CAERNARFON TO PENYGROES

'Carnarvon looks something more than a great fortress planted by a great king as a token of his might and resolution. It seems built to be the palace and dwelling place, as well as the stronghold and rock of defence, of potent princes.' A. G. Bradley from *Highways and Byways in North Wales*

This is one of two rides that feature the Lôn Eifion Cycleway. The cycleway is, in turn, one of three recreational routes provided by Gwynedd Council that are collectively known as the Lonydd Glas Network. The other two are shorter routes and are known as the Lôn Las Ogwen and Lôn Las Menai routes and feature earlier in the book. The Lôn Eifion Cycleway is a particularly enjoyable route as it is completely traffic-free and blessed with unsurpassed views. Facing west you have the sea, to the south there is the Lleyn Peninsula and turning east there are the magnificent mountains of Snowdonia. You will cycle very gently uphill and cross many streams as they flow from the mountains toward the sea. The Lôn Eifion Cycleway is also a very important part of the National Cycle Network Route 8 and runs for 12.5 miles from Caernarfon to the rural village of Bryncir. There are plenty of attractions close to the route that you can explore, including the Glynllifon Country Park, the picturesque Nantlle Valley and its quarries, and the narrow gauge Welsh Highland Railway that initially runs parallel with the cycleway. Further information can be obtained from the 'Gwynedd Recreational Routes' leaflet, published by Gwynedd Council and available from Tourist Information Offices.

BACKGROUND AND PLACES OF INTEREST

Caernarfon Castle
This part of Wales is famous for its mighty castles, which are some of the world's finest. Leading them all is the quartet of castles at Beaumaris, Conwy, Harlech and Caernarfon which are masterpieces of medieval military architecture. Caernarfon was begun in 1283 by Edward I after he had conquered Wales; it was constructed to show military strength and provide a seat of government and a royal palace. The castle is almost unique amongst English castles with its use of polygonal towers and completely so with the use of banded masonry. The magnificent design seems to echo the walls of Constantinople, the imperial power of Rome and a castle of dreams — 'the fairest that ever a man saw' of Welsh myth and legend. Standing at the mouth of the Seiont River, the fortress

Left: The dramatic outline of Caernarfon castle.

dominates the town. In 1969 the castle gained worldwide fame as the setting for the Investiture of HRH Prince Charles as Prince of Wales. There is much for the visitor to enjoy at Caernarfon Castle in addition to being impressed by its sheer size and architectural design. There are walks along the walls as well as imaginative exhibitions contained within the towers. The castle is also home to the Regimental Museum of the Royal Welch Fusiliers, the oldest regiment associated with Wales.

The Welsh Highland Railway

The first part of this ride is alongside the newly built section of the Welsh Highland Railway that runs from Caernarfon to Dinas, the old starting point of the railway. This narrow gauge railway originally linked Porthmadog to Dinas via Aberglaslyn, Beddgelert and Rhyd-Ddu. The section of the line has been reopened by the Festiniog Railway Company and there are ambitious plans to reopen the whole line in stages, back to Porthmadog. (Tel: 01766 512340 for more information.)

Inigo Jones Slateworks

Immediately alongside the cycleway but somewhat hidden away is the Inigo Jones Slateworks, which has a long pedigree. We only found it because they had put an ice cream sign by the cycleway and we went looking. The works were originally opened in 1861 when most of the output was slates for use in schools. Inigo Jones now prefabricates natural Welsh slate into architectural, monumental and craft products. Here you can see craftsman working in this most Welsh of materials and can have a guided tour of the works. The slateworks is open the whole year round. (Tel: 01286 830242 for more information.)

Below: A Welsh Highland Railway locomotive filling up.

Starting Point: From the Welsh Highland Railway station in Caernarfon.

Parking and Toilets: There are several car parks in Caernarfon and I suggest that you park in the vicinity of the castle. We parked in the Tan y Bont car park by the outer wall of the castle. The Castle car park is also very convenient. National Cycle Route 8 runs right past this car park, so it is easy to find your way to the start of the ride.

Distance: 6.8 miles (13.6 miles there and back).

Maps: Ordnance Survey Landranger Sheet 115.

Hills: This is a very easy ride and there are no significant hills.

Surface: The surface varies between compacted dust and tarmac. It is of good quality and often wide enough to cycle two abreast.

Safety: Take great care crossing the A499 road. Apart from this there are no significant hazards.

Roads and Road Crossings: The Lôn Eifion Cycleway is completely off-road. A few lanes are crossed plus the busy A499.

Refreshments: There are many pleasant cafés from which to choose in Caernarfon. There are also some pubs along the route — the Goat Hotel at 3.6 miles, the Llanfair Arms at Groeslon at about 4.8 miles, and the Yr Afr at Penygroes (a very well run pub) at the end of the ride.

Nearest Tourist Information Centre: Oriel

Pendeitsh, Castle Street, Caernarfon LL55 2NA.

Cycle Hire: Cycle Hire, 1 Slate Quay, Caernarfon LL55 2PB (Tel: 01286 676804). Beics Castell, 33 High Street, Caernarfon LL55 1RH (Tel: 01286 677400). Don's Bikes, 47 Pool Street, Caernarfon (Tel: 01286 677727).

ROUTE INSTRUCTIONS

The route is well signposted so very few directions are necessary. Here are a few to keep you on the right track.

1. (0 miles): From the suggested Tan y Bont car park, follow the cycle route sign to the quay by the castle and you will see a sign 'Lon Eifion 300 yards'. Follow this to the Welsh Highland Railway station.

2. (0.4 miles): Leave the road and cycle parallel with the railway line and green fencing.

3. (3.1 miles): Leave the railway and the compacted dust surface behind and enter a narrower stonier track.

4. (3.6 miles): Cross over the busy A499 — take great care. The route changes to a tarmac surface here.

5. (6.8 miles): This section of the ride ends at Penygroes.

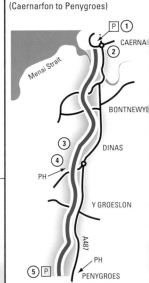

ROUTE 8
LÔN EIFION
(Caernarfon to Penygroes)

Left: Lovely views of the Lleyn Peninsula.

Left: Checking the map.

that other old railway routes in the British Isles have not enjoyed the same good fortune. Enjoy this ride, the Lôn Eifion is a magnificent resource and should be savoured.

Further information can be obtained from the 'Gwynedd Recreational Routes' leaflet, published by Gwynedd Council and available from Tourist Information Offices.

LÔN EIFION
PENYGROES TO BRYNCIR

'I have myself a great affection for this breezy open land of Lleyn; so full of simple rural humanity, so happy, so productive and yet so far removed from the commonplace rectangularity of its sister region of Anglesey.' A. G. Bradley writing on his impressions of the Lleyn Peninsula in his *Highways and Byways in North Wales*

This is one of two rides based on the Lôn Eifion Cycleway, and this one has a more remote setting than the Caernarfon to Penygroes stretch. There are wonderful views of the mountains of the Lleyn Peninsula — the 'Land's End of Wales' — an area that is one of the most important strongholds of Welsh life and customs. The Lôn Eifion Cycleway traces the route of an old railway line. The increase in the use of roads in the 1960s led to the closure of many railway lines in the area. With their disappearance, the land that previously formed the permanent way became the property of the now defunct Caernarfonshire County Council. The 1980s brought an increase in demand for this land for footpaths and cycle use and it slowly became available for these purposes. Caernarfonshire and later Gwynedd Council deserve our thanks for ensuring that these routes became available at such a comparatively early stage — it is such a pity

BACKGROUND AND PLACES OF INTEREST

Penygroes
Penygroes was, until the beginning of this century, the centre of the copper and slate mines, and the remains of this can be seen on the hills to the east. The tradition continues at the Inigo Jones Slateworks which was first opened in 1861 and originally made slates for school use. A wide variety of products is now manufactured. There is a self-guided tour, video on slate-mining and a studio in which visitors can have a go at engraving. (Tel: 01286 830242 for more information.)

Lleyn Peninsula
The Lleyn Peninsula separates Caernarfon Bay from Cardigan Bay. It is a picturesque mix of farming and woodland country with groups of hills and mountains providing dramatic coastal views. The highest hill is Yr Eifl at a striking 1,850ft. It could be said that there are two Lleyns. The first is the coastal one looking out on Cardigan Bay where there are the popular watering-places of Abersoch, Pwllheli and Criccieth. The second is the much quieter inland area which seems to have its own character being mainly quiet and Welsh-speaking. Throughout the many centuries of the Dark Ages and

medieval times the Lleyn was extensively visited by pilgrims travelling to Bardsey Island, off the tip of the peninsula. Reputedly, 20,000 are believed to have died on the island.

Porthmadog

Porthmadog was at one time a busy port mainly serving the Blaenau Ffestiniog stone quarries, and the history of the port is recalled at the Maritime Museum which is open at Easter and from June to September daily (Tel: 01766 513736). Porthmadog is also the home of two railways. The Festiniog Railway reaches Blaenau Ffestiniog after $13^1/_2$ miles and a 1hr journey and provides good coastal and mountain views. It first opened in 1836 as a horse-drawn tramway to service the slate quarries at Blaenau Ffestiniog. It first carried passengers in 1865 and stayed open until 1946. Since then it has been reopened stage by stage since 1954. Both steam and diesel engines are used on the route. There is a daily service (but with a limited winter service) and a museum, shop and restaurant.

The Welsh Highland Railway also has a short length of restored line in operation with about a mile of track from Porthmadog now open. (See the other Lôn Eifion ride for information of restoration at the Caernarfon end.)

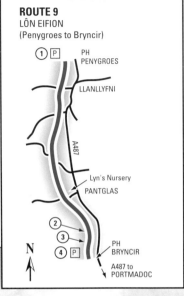

ROUTE 9
LÔN EIFION
(Penygroes to Bryncir)

Above: Penygroes.

Starting Point: From the recommended car park detailed below.

Parking and Toilets: Park in the small car park (nine spaces) opposite the Eifionydd Farmers' Association. There is also a car park at the end of the ride at Bryncir, although be careful if you have bikes on top as it has a height limitation bar.

Distance: 5.6 miles (11.2 miles there and back).

Maps: Ordnance Survey Landranger Sheet 123.

Hills: There are no significant hills on this ride.

Surface: The surface is extremely good and often wide enough for cycling two abreast. It is composed of a mixture of tarmac and compacted dust.

Safety: The surface becomes a little soft and loose in places as you approach Bryncir, so it is advisable to keep your speed down or you could lose your balance.

Roads and Road Crossings: This ride is completely traffic-free. The only roads that are crossed are quiet country lanes and farm tracks.

Refreshments: There is the Yr Afr pub at the start of the ride in Penygroes — an extremely well run pub in which the licensee has taken a great pride. Simple snacks and drinks are available from the quaint Lyn's Nursery at a distance of about 3.8 miles. At the end of the ride there is the Bryncir Arms, although it looked at the time of cycling that it might be closed.

Nearest Tourist Information Centre: Oriel Pendeitsh, Castle Street, Caernarfon LL55 2NA.

Cycle Hire: Cycle Hire, 1 Slate Quay, Caernarfon LL55 2PB (Tel: 01286 676804). Beics Castell, 33 High Street, Caernarfon LL55 1RH (Tel: 01286 677400). Don's Bikes, 47 Pool Street, Caernarfon (Tel: 01286 677727).

ROUTE INSTRUCTIONS
The route is well waymarked so very few directions are necessary, but here are a few hints to keep you on the right track.

1. (0 miles): From the small car park by the Eifionydd Farmers' Association turn left to cycle south on the cycleway.

2. (4.7 miles): Cross a little stream and then a concrete farm drive — at this point you are very close to the A487(T).

3. (5.4 miles): Pass another small stream and track.

4. (5.6 miles): You arrive at the Lôn Eifion Information Board and this marks the end of the traffic-free cycleway. If you wish to enter Bryncir, cycle on for a few yards past the cattle market and auctioneers to find the Bryncir Arms on the main A487(T).

Above: Lôn Eifion information board.

COED Y BRENIN FOREST PARK

A CIRCULAR MOUNTAIN BIKE RIDE FOR NOVICES FROM THE VISITOR CENTRE

'If ever you come to Dolgellau,
Dont stop at the – Hotel,
For there's nothing to put in your belly,
And the waiter dont answer the bell.'
Lines by William Makepeace Thackeray
penned in the visitors' book of an anonymous
hotel in Dolgellau

The Coed y Brenin Forest could be called the
mountain biking centre of Wales and so it is
no surprise that cycling is well provided for
there, where there are five waymarked trails
to choose from. It is wonderful that young
people are being persuaded into the
countryside earlier than in the past, by this
opportunity for adventure and physical
exercise. It will give them a heightened sense
of appreciation as they reach more mature
years. The routes range from the challenge of
The Red Bull Route (the first commercially
sponsored mountain bike ride in the country)
to the Fun Route for novices that is the
subject of this ride. I found the waymarking
on the Fun Route to be extremely good; in
fact it could not be faulted. The route is only 6
miles long, but it does necessitate a
significant amount of uphill work especially at
the beginning. There are two opportunities
for a short cut that provide significant
reductions in the total distance and the
climbing to be done. I would suggest that you
allow 2hr to complete the full ride. Excellent
full colour fold-out leaflets are available from
the visitor centre which show routes for both
mountain biking and walking.

BACKGROUND AND PLACES OF INTEREST

Dolgellau and nearby Cader Idris
I am sure, like me, you will find yourself
asking the question — just how do you
pronounce that word 'Dolgellau'? Well, it was
explained to me that it should be said as Dol-
Gethly. The town is pleasantly positioned on

Above: The start of the ride.

the banks of the Wnion which is spanned by
an attractive 17th-century bridge. To the
south west of Dolgellau is Cader Idris (Chair
of Idris), a spectacular mountain with a very
distinctive shape of perpendicular walls of
rock of some 900ft. If you find yourself
enjoying a climb on that mountain, you must
not on any account spend the night there, as
legend says that you will wake up in the
morning as either a poet or a lunatic. This
southern part of Snowdonia is more homely,
more verdant, than the rugged craggy
treeless land closer to Snowdon. We were
based near Dolgellau for some time during
the writing of this book and stayed at a
farmhouse on the slopes of Cader Idris. Here
we enjoyed what we believe to be the finest
bed and breakfast in Wales — unlike the
unfortunate Mr Thackeray. Only a 5min walk

away was a pub alongside a lake where you could relax on a verandah and enjoy the convivial company of fellow cyclists and walkers or, if you knew how, enjoy an hour or so of fly fishing from a boat.

The Coed y Brenin Forest Park
Most of the forest used to belong to the Nannau Estate whose first owner was Cadougan, the 12th-century Prince of Powys. The land later passed to the Vaughan family, but when the Forestry Commission started planting in the 1920s and 1930s, the name was changed to Coed y Brenin — the Forest of the King — to celebrate the Silver Jubilee of King George V. Aside from mountain biking there is plenty of scope for orienteering and walking. There are four waymarked and themed trails including the Copper Trail and a Gold Mines Trail. In the heart of the forest, signposted from the A470, is the visitor centre which is open daily from Easter to September. This provides a comprehensive interpretation of the many aspects of the forest and includes information on past goldmining activities. (Tel: 01341 422289 for further information.)

Trawsfynydd
Trawsfynydd is a village beside the lake of the same name, which was created in 1930 as part of the Maentwrog hydro-electric scheme. Dominating the scene is a nuclear power station, but this is now closed. If you travel to the junction of the A470/A487, which is just beyond the power station, you will notice a small road which leads off to the east. It is well worth travelling a mile down this road and looking for a tiny Roman amphitheatre which can easily be missed if you are not aware that it is there. This amphitheatre is the only example in Britain of an auxiliary fort used in Roman and Norman times. Just a short distance to the southwest is Tomen-y-Mur (Mound of the Wall). This mound was probably an early Norman motte. This area is also important in Welsh legend as it was said to be the seat of the princes of Ardudwy.

Below: A group of young riders under instruction.

Starting Point: This ride starts from the Coed y Brenin Visitor Centre, which is situated alongside the A470(T), 7 miles north of Dolgellau.

Parking and Toilets: Parking and toilets are available at the visitor centre.

Distance: 6 miles round trip.

Maps: Ordnance Survey Landranger Sheet 124.

Hills: This is a 'novice' mountain bike route, but there are three significant climbs. The first is right at the beginning and having survived that one you should accomplish the other ones easily.

Surface: Most of this ride is off-road on forest tracks. The surface in places tends to consist of loose slate.

Safety: This is the easiest of the rides at Coed y Brenin; nevertheless it needs to be treated with respect as it is in effect a mountain biking route, and I would describe it as demanding. The advice of Forest Enterprise is that the route is not suitable for children under 10 years of age. A mountain bike and cycle helmet are essential for this ride.

Roads and Road Crossings: There is a short section of about ¼ mile that takes place on the drive to the forest centre from the A470(T).

Refreshments: There is a café at the visitor centre. On a fine day it is very pleasant having a picnic sitting on one of the many large rocks in the nearby River Mawddach.

Nearest Tourist Information Centre: Ty Meirion, Eldon Square, Dolgellau LL40 1PU (Tel: 01341 422888).

Supplementary Information Available: There are some excellent Forest Enterprise leaflets giving details of several rides, including this one, that are available from the visitor centre.

ROUTE 10

COED Y BRENIN FOREST PARK

(A circular mountain bike ride for novi from the visitor centre)

Cycle Hire: Bikes are available for hire at the visitor centre from Beics Coed y Brenin (Tel: 01341 440666 day or 01766 540569 evening).

ROUTE INSTRUCTIONS

This ride is one of three fully waymarked routes. It is the easiest of the three and is known as The Fun Route. It is marked with yellow waymarkers both on the ground and on the mountain biking leaflet available from the visitor centre. Detailed instructions are therefore not necessary. Two short cuts are also possible which can reduce the distances from 6 miles to 3 or 5 miles.

1. (0 miles): From the car park start the ride by passing through the Red Bull/Karimoor Arch and start the steep climb up through the forest. Merely follow the yellow waymarkers.

2. (6.0 miles): The ride ends when you return to the visitor centre car park.

Left: Follow the Yellow route.

THE MAWDDACH TRAIL
DOLGELLAU TO BARMOUTH

*'Who long for rest, who look for pleasure
Away from counter, court or school
O where live well your lease of leisure
But here, here at Penmaenpool.'*
Gerald Manley Hopkins, written in 1876

This is an extremely easy ride and very suitable for families with young children as it is completely traffic-free if you start from the Mawddach Trail car park at the junction of the A493 and A470(T) near Dolgellau. The route follows the southern edge of the Mawddach Estuary — acclaimed as one of the most beautiful in Europe — between Dolgellau and Barmouth, along the line of an old railway. The railway ran between Barmouth Junction (which is now known as Morfa Mawddach) and Dolgellau and had a life of exactly 100 years. At the Barmouth end of the trail, cyclists have to pay a small toll to cross the estuary via the timber-built railway bridge — now looking a little shaky as it was built in 1867. Do not confuse this with the wooden road toll bridge which spans the Mawddach at Penmaenpool. Between the railway bridge and Barmouth there is a short distance of ³/₄ mile on roads which, if you have a young family, you may prefer to undertake by wheeling your bikes. The trail is managed by the Snowdonia National Park Authority and forms part of Route 8 of the National Cycle Network.

BACKGROUND AND PLACES OF INTEREST

Mawddach Estuary and Dolgellau
The Mawddach Estuary is now very quiet and is a cyclists' paradise, but at one time it echoed to the sound of shipbuilding and the roar of steam trains. However, it is now managed and protected by the Snowdonia National Park

Right: The Penmaenpool toll bridge.

Authority. The views of the hills surrounding the estuary were striking enough for Wordsworth to describe it as 'this sublime estuary'. Between 1770 and 1827 over 100 boats were built on the Mawddach from the local oak to be found along the estuary. Dolgellau and Barmouth have been closely linked over the centuries and by cycling the Mawddach Trail these links can be explored. The development of the area has been heavily influenced by the natural resources of the surrounding countryside, with oak, gold, slate and wool being predominant. Owen Glendower, the 14th-century Welsh prince, had his parliament house in Dolgellau and the development of the Quaker religion in Wales was centred here in the 17th century. There was much persecution of the Quakers and many emigrated to America, taking their Welsh placenames with them. During the writing of this book, I visited Dolgellau many

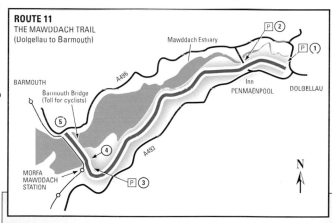

ROUTE 11
THE MAWDDACH TRAIL
(Dolgellau to Barmouth)

times and grew to love the place. Due to the dark stone used to build it and its narrow roads, Dolgellau can be a rather depressing place on a wet day, but on a sunny day its character seems to change out of all recognition. It is an ideal base to discover southern Snowdonia.

Brief History of the Railway

The old railway ran from Barmouth to Ruabon and was opened in 1869. It was a very popular route for Victorian holidaymakers from the northwest of England wishing to visit Barmouth. An interesting example of the potential inefficiencies of private railway operation at the time is illustrated by the fact that Dolgellau had two railway stations on either side of the track with separate staff and signalboxes. The Bala & Dolgellau Railway ran the route from Bala while the Aberystwyth & Welsh Railway were responsible for most of the line from Dolgellau. In 1922 the Great Western Railway swallowed these companies up, and in 1965 the line was closed in common with many others.

Above: The timber railway bridge.

Barmouth and the Fairbourne Small Gauge Railway

The main attraction of this Victorian and sometimes overcrowded resort is the two miles of splendid sands that are separated from the town by the railway line. It has all the expected attractions of a coastal holiday resort that if you have children will part you from your money very quickly. It is also possible to cross the estuary — by ferry only — to Penrhyn Point where the Fairbourne small gauge railway can be found. This is the smallest of Wales's little railways and was originally constructed in the 19th century as a horse-drawn tramway of 2ft gauge to supply materials for the construction of Fairbourne village. It became a 15in gauge railway in 1916 and in recent years has been rescued by enthusiasts. The railway is open from April to September (Tel: 01341 250362 for more information).

Starting Point: From the recommended car park below.

Parking and Toilets: Park in the Mawddach Trail car park which has been specially provided by the Snowdonia National Park Authority for users of the trail. It is also possible to park at Penmaenpool (car park with toilets) and at Morfa Mawddach station (also with toilets).

Distance: 7.8 miles (15.6 miles there and back).

Maps: Ordnance Survey Landranger Sheet 124.

Hills: None.

Surface: Very good grit-based surface of sufficient width to permit two-abreast cycling in most places.

Safety: There are no particular safety hazards.

Roads and Road Crossings: One small road feeding the wooden road toll bridge at Penmaenpool.

Refreshments: The George III Hotel alongside the route at Penmaenpool has a large number of tables outside and the food is good. Otherwise there is Barmouth which is a typical seaside town with typical seaside-town food.

Nearest Tourist Information Centre: Ty Meirion, Eldon Square, Dolgellau LL40 1PU (Tel: 01341 422888).

Cycle Hire: George III Hotel, Penmaenpool, Dolgellau (Tel: 01341 422525). Dragon Bikes 'N' Kites, Smithfield Street, Dolgellau (Tel: 01341 423008).

ROUTE INSTRUCTIONS

1. (0 miles): Negotiate the wooden gate and cattle grid to leave the car park.

2. (1.2 miles): Cross the car park and small road that leads to the road toll bridge; pass the George III Hotel.

3. (6.7 miles): At another car park at Morfa Mawddach, ensure that you continue on the gravelled route close to the toilet (or otherwise you will find yourself on the station platform).

4. (6.9 miles): Join the route alongside the railway line.

5. (7.8 miles): At the end of the bridge, pay your toll and make your way, if you wish, into Barmouth, by turning left to take the road into town.

Below: Enjoying the Mawddach Trail.

THE MONTGOMERY CANAL
WELSHPOOL TO BERRIEW

'Let us pray that this river-like canal will always be preserved along with its attractive cottages, locks and bridges and its tow-path that is such a fine walkers' route through a lovely countryside.' William Condry from his *Exploring Wales*

This stretch of canal provides one of the most peaceful and relaxing rides in this book. After I left Welshpool the canal was a haven of peace and solitude — I met no boats and just two people: a dog walker and a very friendly and helpful British Waterways employee who was cutting the towpath. At the time of writing, none of the canal is officially cycleable. However, there is a phased programme of towpath surfacing which is intended to be complementary with the canal restoration. The section from Frankton to Queen's Head has already been improved and others phases will be commenced — funding permitting. Although cycling on the canal towpath is not currently approved by British Waterways, if you have a permit then the authority will not object, but you are cycling at your own risk. It is important to remember that the towpath surface is generally grassy and is therefore slippery when wet. That being said, this section of the canal has an adequately wide towpath for cycling and, what is more, it is kept very well mowed — an essential prerequisite for a path not in regular use. The ride ends in the particularly lovely village of Berriew which has won best-kept village awards for many years and has good opportunities for refreshment. Cycling permits are obtainable from British Waterways' Ellesmere Office (Tel: 01691 622549).

BACKGROUND AND PLACES OF INTEREST

Montgomery Canal
The canal leaves the Llangollen Canal at Frankton Junction and journeys through Welshpool and on to Newtown for a distance of 35 miles. During this journey it passes from the English county of Shropshire into Powys — that huge county that forms the heart of Wales. Any wayfarer, whether he or she is a cyclist or a walker, who is fortunate enough to follow this watercourse will benefit from the most delightful countryside that England and Wales has to offer, as he or she travels through the Severn Valley accompanied at a distance on both sides by

Below: The lovely village of Berriew.
Welsh Tourist Board

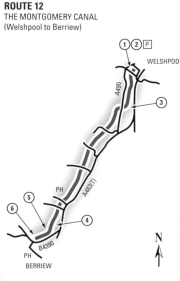

ROUTE 12
THE MONTGOMERY CANAL
(Welshpool to Berriew)

Above: The Powysland Museum and Canal Centre.

long hills of the most pleasant form. The cargo carried on the canal was predominantly coal and limestone and the locks were designed to take a unique form of narrowboat — 11 of these locks enable the descent to the Severn and a further 14 enable a climb along the river valley to Newtown. The canal was finished in 1819 and took 30 years to complete, having been built by three different ventures. In 1850 it became part of the network of the Shropshire Union Railway & Canal Company — decline followed and it became part of the London Midland & Scottish Railway Company in 1923. The canal was legally abandoned, while the country was at war in 1944, by the LMS Act of Parliament. This effectively closed the canal and led to the lowering of many bridges. However, things are now looking very much better, with restoration work having started in 1968 by the Shropshire Union Canal Society and continued with further work funded by the Prince of Wales Committee. Much additional work has been conducted in recent years and the canal is moving gradually towards full reopening.

Powysland Museum
This is a wonderful museum housed in a recently renovated former warehouse immediately alongside the canal in Welshpool. The museum was originally funded by the Powysland Club which is the oldest archaeological society in Great Britain and has maintained continuous published records since 1867. The museum moved to its present site in 1990 and won an award in 1993 for the most improved rural museum. The exhibits portray Montgomeryshire life from earliest prehistoric settlers to the present day. There are also artefacts illustrating the development of the railway and canal systems. The archaeological exhibits include finds made by the earliest members of the Powysland Club; there is also a social history gallery of 19th and 20th century life. This is a wonderful museum in an unexpected place and very much worth a visit. Opening times vary according to the time of year. (Tel: 01938 554656 for more information.)

The Welshpool & Llanfair Railway
This is a narrow (2ft 6in) gauge railway that linked Welshpool to Llanfair Caereinion from 1903 to 1931 for passenger traffic and carried on to 1956 with goods traffic only. The headquarters are at Llanfair Caereinion and the route has been gradually reopened in stages between 1963 and 1981. The route of this country railway meanders through changing scenery, steep hills, quiet farms and a secluded river valley. (Tel: 01938 810441 for further information.)

Starting Point: The car park by Welshpool Wharf. To get there, first find the roundabout by the main railway station, take the exit marked Smithfield Road, bear left after a short distance, go over a bridge with railings and then turn into the car park.

Parking and Toilets: Park in the Welshpool Wharf pay-and-display car park, which is inexpensive.

Distance: 5.5 miles (11 miles there and back).

Maps: Ordnance Survey Landranger Sheets 126 and 136.

Hills: None.

Surface: Mostly grass towpath of generous width and well mown at the time of cycling. Some sections are a little bumpy. Unless all family members are experienced cyclists it would be better to cycle this route in dry weather.

Safety: Care should be taken when cycling under canal bridges as their curved nature could lead to a nasty blow on the head or shoulder. Also, some parts of the towpath can be slippery in wet weather. Although the path is of generous width, emphasise to children the importance of keeping away from the rushes at the edge, otherwise they could get an unpleasant soaking.

Roads and Road Crossings: If you decide to cycle from the canal into Berriew, there is a stretch of about 1¹/₂ miles on a quiet country road.

Refreshments: The Horseshoes Inn about 1 mile before Berriew. In Berriew there is The Lion Hotel & Restaurant and The Talbot.

Nearest Tourist Information Centre: Vicarage Garden Car Park, Welshpool SY21 7DD (Tel: 01938 552043).

ROUTE INSTRUCTIONS
1. (0 miles): From the car park, cross the canal by the cast-iron bridge which once carried the Welshpool & Llanfair Railway, turn right to climb down the steps to join the canal towpath.

2. (0.2 miles): Pass the Montgomery Canal Centre, continue on the lane past the builders' merchants and then descend to the towpath (indicated as Severn Way).

3. (1.0 miles): Although the canal looks as if it goes straight on here, you need to turn right under the A490 (Bridge 120).

4. (4.8 miles): At Berriew Lock, the lady who lives in the lock-keeper's cottage has incorporated the towpath into her garden and expressed the view that cyclists should walk this short section!

5. (4.9 miles): Leave the towpath when you are at Bridge 128 by climbing the steepish path, leaving by the wooden gate and turning right to take the country road into Berriew.

6. (5.5 miles): The ride terminates in Berriew.

Below: A milepost along the Montgomery Canal.

THE KERRY RIDGEWAY
A HILLTOP RIDE FROM BISHOP'S CASTLE TO THE PICNIC SITE AT BLOCK WOOD NEAR KERRY

*'In places this road is motorable.
Other parts of it are mere tracks through fields,
moorland or forest.'* William Condry from
Exploring Wales

When I first heard of the village of Kerry and
the Kerry Ridgeway, I assumed that it must
be in Ireland as I was unaware of the Welsh
village of Kerry. This is a delightful hilltop
ride that follows an ancient ridgeway which
for most of its length traces the
English/Welsh Border. These borderlands
are known as Marcher Country, the term
being derived from the ancient word for
marker or boundary, possibly from King
Offa's great 8th-century earthwork, now
known as Offa's Dyke. The area has a feeling
of relaxation about it; a land of hill forts,
wooded valleys and a patchwork of fields, and
yet at various times it has been a land of
conflict as evidenced by the line of castles
built by the powerful Marcher Lords who
fought over this border area. It is a ridgeway
route similar to one that you would expect to
find across a chalk downland ridge in
southern England — the Wiltshire Ridgeway
and the South Downs Way being examples.
The ride starts in England and finishes in
Wales. The route is a mixture of surfaced
byways and unsurfaced bridleways some of
which are effectively field paths. Nowhere will
you find it labelled as the Kerry Ridgeway
except on the Ordnance Survey map. It is
used much more for walking than cycling but
parts of it do make very pleasant cycling.
However, there are two sections where the
bridleway takes the form of a path across a
field and it can be difficult to get along. The
Kerry Ridgeway stretches for a total of 15½
miles from Bishop's Castle in the east to
Cider House Farm in the west. I chose to ride
it from the beginning at Bishop's Castle and
went as far as the picnic site in Block Wood.
The disadvantage of this is the very long
steady climb of about 2 miles out of Bishop's
Castle. It is possible to avoid this by driving to
perhaps Point 2 (Bishop's Moat) and starting
your ride from this point, although there are
no formal parking facilities there. Similarly, if
you only go so far as Point 10 in Long
Plantation you would still have a reasonable
ride but you would avoid one of the sections
across fields (between Kerry Pole and Block
Wood). A leaflet on the Kerry Ridgeway that
provides additional historical background and
describes the route — mainly with the walker
in mind — has been published by Powys
County Council.

Below: Clun Castle.

BACKGROUND AND PLACES OF INTEREST

The Kerry Ridgeway

This fine example of a ridgeway follows the top of the Kerry Hills and is also sometimes known as 'The Castle Road' or 'Yr Hen Ffordd' (the old road). There are so many archaeological features along the route that you feel that you are journeying through both history and prehistory. There are ditches and a dyke, a Norman motte and bailey and prehistoric defensive earthworks. The ditches were built across the ridge roads in the Dark Ages to protect the lowlands of the east against cattle raiders from the higher land to the west. When you look at them today as you ride the route, you will wonder why they could not simply be walked around, but they make more sense if you picture the ridgeway as the only route through impenetrable scrub and swamp. About halfway along the ride, just inside England, can be found the interestingly-named Cantlin Stone. The origin of the name is not clear and there are several legends about its erection. One of them recounts that a traveller died whilst walking the Ridgeway and an argument between the neighbouring parishes of Kerry and Bettws-y-Crwyn about burial of the body occurred. The unfortunate traveller was eventually buried in Bettws-y-Crwyn church and the stone was erected to detail the place where the body

was found. Another version is that it marks the place of the burial of someone named Cantlin thought to have taken place in 1691. The stone features an Ionic cross which is thought to be of Victorian origin but the reason for the cross is again unknown and it could even have been a folly.

Offa's Dyke

A mile or so before Pantglas, Offa's Dyke can be seen. Offa was a Mercian King who lived from AD757 to 796. The Dyke once formed the England/Wales border and extends for a total distance of an incredible 149 miles from Sedbury on the River Severn through to Prestatyn on the north coast. The earthwork is currently evident on the ground for 81 miles. It is an earth bank, usually with one ditch most commonly on the west side but occasionally on both, and with an average height of six feet above ground level. Its main purpose was as a frontier between Mercia and the Welsh Kingdoms and to control trade by confining routes across the border to defined ways through the earthwork. It may also have had a defensive purpose and again may have deterred cattle raiders from the west.

Bishop's Castle and Clun

Bishop's Castle is a small attractive town set on the border of Wales and England and steeped in history. The origins of Bishop's Castle go back as far as the 12th century when a stone castle was built here by the Bishops of Hereford. Little evidence remains of the castle, which was situated at the top of the steep High Street, except that it gave the town its name. If you walk from the castle down the High Street you will pass several medieval buildings including The House on Crutches Museum. The Clun villages and the River Clun are A. E. Housman country and it was him, in his collection of poetry — *A Shropshire Lad* — that gave familiarity to the lines about Clunton, Clunbury, Clungunford and Clun being the quietest places under the sun. Clun is indeed smaller and quieter than Bishop's Castle with an interesting and ancient packhorse bridge and an impressive ruined castle.

Left: Bishop's Castle.

Starting Point: The ride starts from the post office at the centre of Bishop's Castle, which is situated close to the A488 between Shrewsbury and Knighton.

Parking and Toilets: There are two car parks in Bishop's Castle. One is in Harvey Jenkins Street and the other one in Auction Yard contains a public toilet.

Distance: 12.3 miles (24.6 miles there and back).

Maps: Ordnance Survey Landranger Sheets 136 and 137.

Hills: As this is a ridgeway route you first have to climb to the top of the ridge. Unfortunately, this means that the start of the ride is a steady and strenuous climb for over 2 miles.

Surface: This varies between tarmacadam public roads, unsurfaced bridleways and grassy field paths. On the unsurfaced bridleways there are likely to be some deep puddles after wet weather.

Safety: There are no particular hazards associated with this ride.

Roads and Road Crossings: About 11 miles of this ride is traffic-free with the remainder on public roads. However, these roads are quiet country lanes where you only meet the occasional vehicle so they are essentially safe.

Refreshments: The only possibility of refreshment is at the start or end of the ride in Bishop's Castle. We took a picnic and had it at the end of the outward leg at the picnic site on the B4368. Another alternative would be to stop for a picnic in Long Plantation.

Nearest Tourist Information Centre: Bishop's Castle Tourist Information Centre,

Old Time, 29 High Street, Bishop's Castle, Shropshire SY9 5BE (Tel: 01588 638467).

Cycle Hire: Longmynd Cycles, Church Stretton (Tel: 01694 722367) and Terry's Cycles, Church Stretton (Tel: 01694 723302).

ROUTE INSTRUCTIONS

1. (0 miles): Proceed straight up the High Street toward the clock tower and pass to the left of the tower using the cobbled path. Turn left into Welsh Street which soon becomes a country lane with high banks on either side.

2. (2.3 miles): At a junction of routes, take the route signposted 'Pantglas 3, Hopton 4'.

3. (3.8 miles): By the telephone box (close to Dog and Duck Cottage), carry straight on.

4. (5.2 miles): At Pantglas (a farm just after the second turning to Cwm) bear left onto a lesser road. This point is best identified by a large dark-coloured grain silo and a number of black corrugated farm buildings.

5. (6.4 miles): Pass through a seven-bar steel gate. The track runs across a field initially between a row of stunted trees (predominantly hawthorn) and the right-hand edge of the field, which later becomes two rows of stunted trees.

6. (6.6 miles): Pass through a further steel bar gate.

7. (6.7 miles): Pass through a third steel bar gate to leave this field section to rejoin a trackway again.

8. (7.2 miles): The route becomes a tarmac one. Be careful here as you could easily take the wrong direction. Stay on the surfaced section for only a few yards before you turn

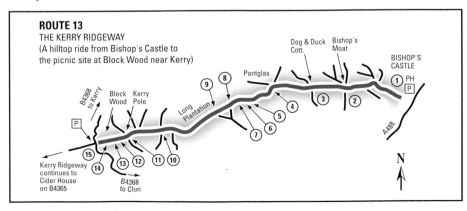

ROUTE 13
THE KERRY RIDGEWAY
(A hilltop ride from Bishop's Castle to the picnic site at Block Wood near Kerry)

off right to cycle down the right-hand side of a felled forestry plantation.

9. (7.8 miles): You will enter a plantation of large spruce trees and will reach a fork. Take the left hand option — you are now on a gravelled forest track.

10. (10.0 miles): The route becomes a tarmac surface.

11. (11.3 miles): The road meets a T-junction by the farm settlement known as Kerry Pole. Leave the road by proceeding straight on through the rusty six-bar metal gate onto a bridleway which runs along the right-hand side of the field.

12. (11.5 miles): Pass through a wooden gate between fields.

13. (11.7 miles): Pass through a further five-bar gate to leave the fields and join a defined track again — you are now accompanied by Block Wood on your right.

14. (12.0 miles): In Block Wood, pass through a further wooden bar gate to join a gravelled surface.

15. (12.3 miles): Arrive at the picnic spot by the B4368 which marks the end of the ride.

Below: Fine views from the ridgeway.

THE ELAN VALLEY TRAIL
A RIDE AROUND FOUR RESERVOIRS FROM THE ELAN VALLEY VISITOR CENTRE

'And when that is all completed, and the mountains of Cwm Dauddwr and of Drygan and Pen-y-Gorllwyn look down upon these miles of lakes and share their ancient solitudes with the silence of unmolested waters, may you and I, dear reader, be alive to come here again and behold a spectacle upon whose possibilities I dare not venture to enlarge.' A. G. Bradley writing in his *Highways and Byways in South Wales* before the Elan Valley Reservoirs were completed

After completion, the Elan Valley Trail will be a route for both walkers and cyclists that will run from the visitor centre to the head of the Penygarreg Reservoir — a distance of nearly 6 miles. The section along the northern edge of the Penygarreg Reservoir already exists in the form of a bridleway. At the time of writing, the section along the eastern edge of the Garreg-ddu Reservoir is under construction and will be complete by the time this book is published. The section from the visitor centre to the Garreg-ddu Reservoir is currently for walkers only but will soon be converted to dual use; again hopefully this will be complete

by the time of publication. There are long-term plans to extend the trail right back to Rhayader. The trail follows the old trackway of the Birmingham Corporation Waterworks Railway which ran for five miles from the visitor centre to the dam at Craig Goch, alongside the Caban-coch, Garreg-ddu and Penygarreg Reservoirs. The purpose of the railway was to facilitate the construction of the dams of the Elan Valley. At Penygarreg Reservoir you will see a cutting that has been blasted through a massive rock. The blasting of this cutting delayed the construction of the railway for three months. This is true wilderness country of man-made lakes edged by smooth rolling hills — it is, in my view, the best lake scenery in Wales. As you travel north on the ride the views get even better with Penygarreg Reservoir with its picturesque island, and culminating with the remote Craig Goch Reservoir. This countryside is also one of the last remaining homes of the red kite in the United Kingdom. You are sure to have a ride to remember.

BACKGROUND AND PLACES OF INTEREST

The Elan Valley Reservoirs
The building of these wonderful dams and reservoirs took place between 1892 and 1904. During the main building period over 5,000 men were employed and over the whole period a total of 50,000 men are recorded as having worked on the project. The reservoirs were built to supply Birmingham and the water travels $73^1/_2$ miles by pipeline to reach its destination. The reservoirs have also served the local area and parts of South Wales in times of shortage. The Elan Valley Reservoirs consist of a string of four narrow lakes running north-south and the original flooding of the valley provided the basis for Francis Brett Young's novel — *The House under the Water.* Sometimes, if the water levels are low (although not visible from this ride) — you can see at the southern end of Caban-coch Reservoir the garden walls of

Left: The dam at Penygarreg Reservoir.

Nant Gwyllt where Shelley lived for a short time after his unfortunate marriage to Harriet Westbrook in 1812. It is also the house that inspired Francis Brett Young's novel.

The Elan Valley Visitor Centre

This is a large centre at the foot of Caban-coch Reservoir, run by Welsh Water and situated 3 miles from Rhayader. It has recently been extended and now contains a café, shop, education room and a well-produced audio visual display. There is also an excellent interpretative exhibition telling the story of how the dams were built and where you can learn the technicalities of how the water is eventually delivered to the consumer. There are extensive picnic facilities close to the centre alongside the attractive River Elan. Other facilities on offer are weekend breaks, Land Rover safaris and guided walks — contact the Ranger's Office for more information (Tel: 01597 810898). The centre is open from mid-March until the end of October (Tel: 01597 810880).

Rhayader

The proper name of Rhayader is Rhaiadr Gwy — the falls of the Wye. There is no 'Rhaiadr' worth speaking of now in this lovely old market town, as the building of the bridge foundations in 1780 removed that notable feature. It is though, surrounded by wild hills and mountains and could perhaps be described as a typical Welsh market town with its charming pubs bulging with farmers on sale days. In addition to the Elan Valley Lakes, there are two notable sites of interest for visitors close by. Situated just to the east of the town on the A44 is the Welsh Royal Crystal Factory where glass blowers demonstrate their skills in front of the kiln and crystal cutters work on their lathes. There is also a well-stocked factory shop. The factory is open on Monday, Tuesday, Thursday and Friday and the shop is open on all days of the week (Tel: 01597 811005 for more information). Gigrin Farm is situated south of the town on the A470(T) and is a working hill farm and Red Kite Feeding Centre, which offers a farm trail and a picnic and a play area (Tel: 01597 810243).

Right: The Elan Valley Visitor Centre.

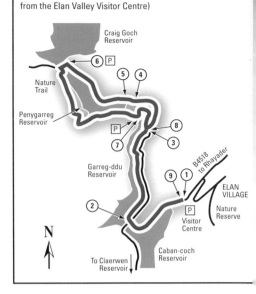

ROUTE 14
THE ELAN VALLEY TRAIL
(A ride around four reservoirs from the Elan Valley Visitor Centre)

Starting Point: This ride starts from the Elan Valley Visitor Centre.

Parking and Toilets: Park in the visitor centre car park where there are toilets. There is also a very convenient car park and toilet at the halfway point at the foot of the Craig Goch Reservoir.

Distance: 11.8 miles.

Maps: Ordnance Survey Landranger Sheet 147.

Hills: None, apart from the initial climb from the visitor centre to the ride.

Surface: The surface on the traffic-free sections is good and consists of hard-packed stone.

Safety: There are no specific safety hazards on this ride. Care is obviously needed with the on-road sections. Also, you will need to bear in mind that this ride approaches an altitude of over 300m so the weather can

change very quickly. Make sure that you listen to a weather forecast and take the appropriate clothing with you, as there is little shelter available.

Roads and Road Crossings: There are two sections of about 1½ and 2½ miles that are 'on road'. The road is a quiet country one and traffic moves slowly, and it provides very pleasant cycling. The first section will disappear when the Elan Valley Trail is completed in the near future. The second can be eliminated if you wish, by undertaking a 'there and back' route alongside the northern shore of Penygarreg Reservoir rather than a circular route using the road for the return.

Refreshments: The only possibility of refreshment en route is a snack van that trades at the Craig Goch Dam at certain times. My advice is to take a picnic and possibly stop at the halfway point of the ride at the foot of the Craig Goch Reservoir, although you will find picturesquely sited picnic tables wherever the route lies close to the water. There are also good facilities at the beginning (and end) of the ride at the visitor centre.

Nearest Tourist Information Centre: Elan Valley Visitor Centre, Elan Valley, near Rhayader LD6 5HP (Tel: 01597 810898).

Cycle Hire: During March to October, mountain bikes are available from the visitor centre (Tel: 01597 810898).

ROUTE INSTRUCTIONS

1. (0 miles): Currently the trail for cyclists starts at Garreg-ddu Reservoir. To get there from the visitor centre you have to either cycle out of the car park back along the entrance drive to join the road or wheel the bikes up the steep steps at the rear of the centre. We decided upon the latter course. Having arrived at the top, you need to lift your bike over the steel fence to cycle on the road. (Plans are in hand to extend the trail for cyclists from the visitor centre to Garreg-ddu, and it may only be necessary to follow a waymarked trail when the ride is undertaken.)

2. (1.4 miles): Avoid the turning left to Claerwen Dam, but instead of taking the 'mountain road to Aberystwyth', pass through the steel gates and then a wooden gate to join the Elan Valley Trail for cyclists which runs along the eastern side of Garreg-ddu Reservoir, parallel with and below the road.

3. (3.2 miles): At the wooden barrier marking the diagonal intersection of the trail with the road, cross to the lower of the two possible routes, on the other side of the road.

4. (4.1 miles): Pass through the wooden gate to cycle along the north eastern bank of the Penygarreg Reservoir.

5. (4.2 miles): Avoid the route which climbs an incline on the right and pass through the wooden gate to continue on the Elan Valley Trail.

6. (5.6 miles): Having arrived at the head of the Penygarreg Reservoir and the foot of the Craig Goch Reservoir, turn left across the road which passes over the dam and then take the road left signposted 'Rhayader 9 miles'.

7. (8.0 miles): Follow the road around a sharp left bend to cross the bridge at the outlet of the Penygarreg Reservoir to continue to follow the road along the eastern side of the Garreg-ddu Reservoir.

8. (8.6 miles): You will meet the point where the Elan Valley Trail crosses the road (outgoing route Point 3); here rejoin the trail for your return to the visitor centre.

9. (11.8 miles): Arrive back at the visitor centre.

THE CLAERWEN RESERVOIR
A RIDE ALONG THE NORTHERN SHORE OF THE RESERVOIR TO CLAERWEN

'But no roads to speak of, save the single one alluded to, penetrate this South Wales wilderness. It can be adventured only on foot or horseback. I have never seen or heard of any strangers from outside Wales engaging in such an enterprise. A. G. Bradley as he was describing the area in his *Highways and Byways in South Wales*

If you enjoy cycle rides where you are unlikely to meet another human being of any description let alone a car, then you will enjoy this one. This is remote country where peace and solitude are yours to be found. The Claerwen Reservoir is surrounded by the most beautifully green upland hills, which to the modern eye are completely unspoilt, although the reader should not forget that the hand of man has created the scene that lies before you. Was it even more beautiful, before the reservoirs were created, when A. G. Bradley described the Afon Claerwen as 'following a tortuous path into a sea of mountains, dark in shadow or green in sunlight or grey with distance'? There are plans to make this route an extension of the National Cycle Network. At the moment there is only a right of way for cycles from the Claerwen Dam to about $3/4$ mile beyond Claerwen — an interesting isolated farmhouse and outbuildings whose history I wish I could relate but of which I know nothing. The route onward from there for about 1 mile is shown as a 'white road' on the OS Landranger map and a right of way over this section for cyclists is currently under discussion with the landowner. This would then make it possible to penetrate the wilderness between Rhayader and Ffair-Rhos, thereby usefully linking the two alternative routes of the National Cycle Network between Builth Wells and Machynlleth.

BACKGROUND AND PLACES OF INTEREST

The Elan Valley Visitor Centre
This is a large centre at the foot of Caban-coch Reservoir, run by Welsh Water and situated 3 miles from Rhayader. Fuller details are given in the previous section (Tel: 01597 810880 for general information).

Below: Claerwen Reservoir

Claerwen Reservoir

The area surrounding the Claerwen and Elan Reservoirs is part of the 70sq mile Elan Estate where, unusually, there is open access guaranteed by a special Act of Parliament. The Claerwen Dam was built later than the Elan Valley Dams. It took six years to build, was finished in 1952 and was opened by HM Queen Elizabeth II. It is nearly 4 miles long and is aligned in an east-west direction. The meandering line of the northern shore of the reservoir, with its frequent feeder streams and the promontories that arise, makes it the most beautiful of all the lakes on the Elan Estate.

Strata Florida Abbey

Strata Florida — the Vale of Flowers — lies to the west of Claerwen and the Elan Valley Estate, and can be reached by a mountain road from the visitor centre which provides a very scenic drive. It is a Cistercian abbey and like many of their establishments is built in a wild and lonely place. The abbey was originally founded in 1164 and became an influential centre of Welsh culture in the 12th and 13th centuries. In 1238 it was the site of an assembly of Welsh princes called by Llewellyn the Great to swear allegiance to his

Above: Claerwen farmhouse.

son Dafydd. The abbey is the burial site of many medieval Welsh princes and the most famous medieval poet — Dafydd ap Gwilym. The main source of income of the abbey was from wool obtained from sheep that grazed on the estates that extended as far east as Rhayader. The Owen Glendower troubles saw the abbey abandoned except for use as military stabling. After the Dissolution, the estate was held by several different owners and passed to the Crown in 1931.

Gigrin Nature Trail and Red Kite Feeding Centre

Situated south east of Rhayader on the A470(T), this is one of the local feeding centres established with the support of the RSPB for the protection of the red kite, where from special hides you can watch young kites feeding on a nearby meadow every day between mid-October to mid-April. There is also a converted barn where there is a video presentation from a camera overlooking a nest showing superb footage of young chicks (Tel: 01597 810243 for more information).

Starting Point: The ride starts from the small 'lay-by' car park at the top of the Claerwen Dam.

Parking and Toilets: There is also a larger car park and toilets at the base of the dam.

Distance: 6.3 miles (12.6 miles there and back).

Maps: Ordnance Survey Landranger Sheet 147.

Hills: There are several streams feeding the reservoir. You cross each one via a bridge, after which there is usually a short stiff climb.

Surface: Generally good. It is basically hard-packed stone, but there are some pot-holes. The use of a mountain bike would be advisable.

Safety: You will need to be careful of the surface which is rough in places. Also, bear in mind that this reservoir is at an altitude of around 300m so the weather can change very quickly. Make sure that you listen to a weather forecast and take the appropriate clothing with you, as there is absolutely no shelter available.

Roads and Road Crossings: Legally this track is a Byway Open to All Traffic (BOAT), so it is theoretically possible to meet vehicles along the way. In practice, the route is likely to be used only by farmers and their Land Rovers. When I rode the route in August I came across one parked car, one Land Rover and two cyclists.

Refreshments: You are strongly advised to take some food and have a picnic along the shore of the reservoir. This is remote country and there is no opportunity for refreshments en route.

Nearest Tourist Information Centre: Elan Valley Visitor Centre, Elan Valley, near Rhayader LD6 5HP (Tel: 01597 810898).

Cycle Hire: During March to October, mountain bikes are available from the visitor centre (Tel: 01597 810898).

ROUTE INSTRUCTIONS

This ride takes you along the northern shore of the reservoir using an old byway. The route is straightforward and no directions are

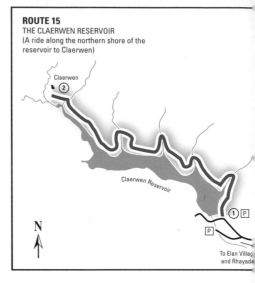

ROUTE 15
THE CLAERWEN RESERVOIR
(A ride along the northern shore of the reservoir to Claerwen)

Claerwen

Claerwen Reservoir

N

To Elan Village
and Rhayader

necessary. Currently there are no rights for cycling beyond Claerwen, although there are plans to establish a right of way ultimately through to Ffair-Rhos.

1. (0 miles): Cycle along the right-hand (north) side of the reservoir.

2. (6.3 miles): Arrive at Claerwen (solitary farm buildings at the head of the reservoir where it is fed by the Afon Claerwen). It is possible to pass over the wooden bridge and use the byway for a further mile until the right of way peters out. Unfortunately, this section is badly drained and you may experience severe ground water up to calf height in places, so my advice is to end your journey at Claerwen and have a leisurely picnic before your return to Claerwen Dam.

Below: Claerwen Dam

THE MONMOUTHSHIRE & BRECON CANAL
NEWPORT TO CWMBRAN

'Mole catchers were employed to protect the canal from moles, rabbits and burrowing animals that posed a serious threat to the canal and to the people who lived close to it by weakening banks or even making breaches in the waterway.' Fourteen Locks Canal Centre Leaflet

Although this ride is for the most part along what remains of the towpath of the Monmouthshire & Brecon Canal between Newport and Cwmbran, it will soon be part of the National Cycle Network Link (Route 46). This will follow the canal and also an old mineral railway line from Newport through Cwmbran and Pontypool and on to Abergavenny and will also include the picturesque Garndiffaith Viaduct and Clydach Gorge. The section that passes through the unitary authority of Torfaen is also known as the Torfaen Cycleway and forms part of the Greater Gwent Cycling Strategy. The ride initially shares the same route as Route 17, but instead of taking the spur canal that went to Risca and Crumlin in Gwent's western valley, it follows the 'main' route of the Monmouth Canal toward Pontnewydd. Unfortunately, as the 'new town' of Cwmbran is approached, bridges have been removed and the canal has been culverted so that not only do several roads have to be crossed, but the canal fizzles out in places. These 'missing' sections will in time be replaced with new off-road cycleway or traffic-calmed routes as part of the work associated with the National Cycle Network. The canal is very picturesque as you leave Newport and the M4, with delicately quaint bridges that connect fields

Below: The River Usk at low tide.

on either side of the canal and do not look strong enough to carry a tractor. There are deep locks which are shuttered and not operational but at least allow the remaining parts of the canal to hold water.

BACKGROUND AND PLACES OF INTEREST

The Monmouth Canal

I have provided some history of the Monmouth Canal in the other rides associated with this canal (Routes 17 and 18). Here I would like to give some background on the boats that were exclusive to this particular canal as they were significantly different from narrow boats on other canals. They were not highly decorated like their counterparts and it was not the practice for owners to live on their boats — they only slept on them when the need arose. In general the boats were open and not covered, as the majority of loads were of a mineral nature and would not be affected by exposure, although cloths could be used to cover anything that might be damaged. The boats were 60ft in length and $8^1/_2$ft in width and normally constructed of elm and oak with very short chimneys — a design constraint caused by the many low bridges spanning the canal. It was normal practice to feed the horses at regular places along the canal bank and they would stubbornly stop and not move on until their nosebags were filled. The horses were reshod every two weeks and special shoes were used to provide a good grip on the towpath and get the boat under way. The

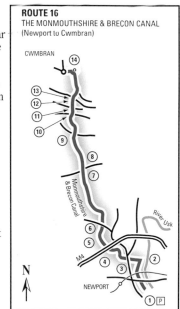

ROUTE 16
THE MONMOUTHSHIRE & BRECON CANAL
(Newport to Cwmbran)

Above: Old dock shunting locomotive — Newport.

bargees generally owned the horses, although they often bought them from the canal company by instalments. This information is based on an interesting leaflet which is available from the Fourteen Locks Canal Centre at Rogerstone on the Crumlin arm of the canal (Tel: 01633 894802).

Caerleon

Very close to Newport is the old Roman stronghold of Caerleon. Originally this fortress was known as Isca (after the River Usk), but became known to the Welsh as Caerleon which was a shortened form of Castra Legionis — simply the fort of the legion. There were normally 5-6,000 men of the 2nd Augustan Legion stationed here and they stayed until late in the 4th century. At first their protection was provided by earth and timber but by the end of the first century the fortress was made of stone. The wealth that accompanied the garrison ensured that a settlement gradually grew up outside of the walls and this developed into a town. Legend has it that in the immediate post-Roman period Arthur was crowned and had his capital here and the amphitheatre became known as King Arthur's Round Table. The amphitheatre was built around AD90 and could seat the whole legion of 6,000 soldiers. In addition to the amphitheatre there are the barracks and the baths to be seen. The baths are especially noteworthy. They were only discovered in 1964 but have been excavated and provided with excellent visitor facilities. They are probably the most complete example of a bath of this type in the British Isles. The Legionary Museum is open daily throughout the year, with the precise times depending upon season (Tel: 01633 423134).

Blaenavon Ironworks

Built in 1788, the ironworks were in their heyday in the 1820s, and it was in 1876 that Gilchrist Thomas solved how to separate phosphorus from iron. The works now stand as a ruin, although they are one of Europe's best preserved examples. The viewing platform enables the visitor to see the blast furnaces, casting houses, water balance lift and workers' houses. The works are open during the summer months (Tel: 01495 752036 for more information). In St Peter's Church, Blaenavon, there are several iron artefacts, notably an iron font and iron gravestones and also memorials to the industrial pioneers.

Starting Point: From the Riverway car park — see below.

Parking and Toilets: Park in the Riverway car park which as its name implies is alongside the River Usk on the west bank. This is a long-stay pay-and-display car park with reasonable charges. Toilets are available in nearby Newport town centre, which you can reach by the covered elevated walkway from the car park.

Distance: 7 miles (14 miles there and back).

Maps: Ordnance Survey Landranger Sheet 171.

Hills: There is only one hill as you climb past the five locks section.

Surface: The towpath is wide and surfaced for the most part with a stone base and a gritty top dressing.

Safety: Care should be taken when cycling under the charming little canal bridges as their curved nature and narrowing of the towpath could lead to a nasty blow on the head or shoulder or a thorough wetting.

Roads and Road Crossings: There are several crossings of minor roads. There is about 1½ miles of road work to do if you wish to travel from the end of the canal ride into Cwmbran.

Refreshments: The only opportunities for refreshment are in Newport or Cwmbran. My advice is to do as I did and take a picnic on this particular ride.

Nearest Tourist Information Centre: Museum and Art Gallery, John Frost Square, Newport NP9 1HZ (Tel: 01633 842962).

ROUTE INSTRUCTIONS

Getting to the canal at Barrack Hill from the Riverway car park is an intricate affair as you have to cross the busy main roads connecting Newport to the north and M4. Fortunately, subways and elevated walkways have been provided and the canal can be accessed without exposure to heavy traffic.

1. (0 miles): From the Riverway car park, follow the paved way past the Steel Wave sculpture toward the castle ruin. Pass under the road and rail bridges that cross the River Usk by dismounting and turning left into the subway tunnel then right into another subway tunnel and then taking a short 'wooden causeway' through the old castle ruin before continuing to follow the river bank. You will pass the side of Sainsbury's that most customers never see, and then through some silver birch trees.

2. (0.8 miles): You will see a recreational park on the left, swing left here to position the park on your right and join a quiet residential street (Evans Street) and at the end, by the Old Rising Sun, dismount to cross Lyne Road to the pub side and continue along this road to the Spar Shop and Boilermakers Club. Here turn left and pass the Coronation Working Men's Club. Pass under the elevated concrete roads to gain access to the elevated pedestrian crossing which you should use to cross the road and stream below safely.

3. (1.3 miles): Ah, relief, as the elevated crossing delivers you to the start of the canal at Barrack Hill, where you can at last follow the quiet towpath.

4. (1.8 miles): The canal forks here. Avoid going over the ramp and instead turn right around the ramp, under the motorway following the white arrows, through the plate metal gate onto the towpath.

5. (2.1 miles): Swing left over the bridge and adjoining lock.

6. (2.4 miles): Cross a fairly busy road.

7. (3.9 miles): Cross a further road.

8. (4.2 miles): At the 'five locks section' the route is fairly steep.

9. (4.9 miles): Cross a traffic-calmed road — the towpath changes to the other side of the canal here.

10. (5.3 miles): Cross a further road.

11. (5.5 miles): The canal has been culverted here. Cross the road — by the Nursery and Parks Depot — take the road opposite for about 100yd and rejoin the tarmac towpath on the left of the canal.

12. (5.7 miles): The towpath merges into Broadweir Road, cross a small lane and rejoin the towpath on the right of the canal.

13. (5.8 miles): This section of the canal towpath ends in Commercial Street by the Halfway Pub, alongside the main A4051 sunk in a cutting on your right. If you wish to find your way into Cwmbran town centre, turn right over the bridge and then left to follow the signs into the centre.

14. (7.0 miles): Arrive at Cwmbran town centre.

Left: A peaceful approach to Cwmbran.

THE MONMOUTHSHIRE AND BRECON CANAL
NEWPORT TO THE PRINCE OF WALES CANALSIDE PUB AT RISCA

'Leggers were sometimes employed to take narrow boats through tunnels through which towpaths were not constructed. The leggers lay across the width of the boat and "walked" on the canal sides or ceiling to propel it slowly through the tunnel. Fourteen Locks Canal Centre Leaflet

This ride takes you along the west bank of the River Usk, across Newport to join the canal at Barrack Hill. From here it runs parallel with the M4 and then strikes northwest to Risca and ends at a favourite stopping place for cyclists — the Prince of Wales pub alongside the canal. The towpath is to form part of the initial 2,500 miles of Britain's National Cycle Network, known as the Celtic Trail. The trail is designated as Route 4 of the network, and will run from Newport to Kidwelly — a total of 186 miles. At least 70% of the trail will be off-road and will run in proximity to the major centres of population and tourism, linking local communities with safe and continuous paths.

Although at first sight the canal appears to be functional as it is 'in water', it soon becomes apparent that the lock gates have been replaced with concrete shutters, which at least retain the water for some recreational uses. However, since the closure of this branch of the canal in 1949 many bridges have been removed and the canal culverted, so it is necessary to cross several minor roads during the ride.

BACKGROUND AND PLACES OF INTEREST

The Monmouth Canal and Fourteen Locks Centre

If you examine a Landranger Ordnance Survey map, you will find that the canal from Brecon to Newport and from Pontywaun to Newport are both identified as the Monmouthshire & Brecon Canal. This tends to mislead as these waterways were originally built as two separate concerns. This ride takes place on the Monmouth Canal which itself divides into two arms. The main arm of the Monmouth Canal ran for 11 miles from Newport to Pontnewydd — a section of this is covered in Route 16. (The canal that joined the Monmouth Canal near Pontnewydd to Brecon was built later as the separate Brecon & Abergavenny Canal.) This ride is based on the second arm of the Monmouth Canal that starts at Crumlin and joins the main Monmouth Canal at Crindau just north of Newport. This Crumlin Arm descends 358ft by 12 simple locks, a flight of five locks near Newport and an amazing flight of 14 locks, weirs and counter-balancing ponds near Rogerstone. Many tramways were built to serve the canal system and these were often up to seven miles long and would enable horse-drawn trams to convey products to the barges. The economic importance of the canal can be judged by looking at one particular year (1798) when 44,000 tons of goods were carried, although in its heyday twice that amount was transported. Iron, coal and timber were taken to Newport and shop goods, stone and iron ore filled the barges on the return journey. Income for the canal was derived from a system of tolls and the rate due was dependent upon the cargo that was carried. Iron and merchandise attracted 5d

Left: The Steel Wave sculpture, Newport.

per ton per mile; ironstone, ore, coal and limestone attracted $2^1/_2$d per ton per mile and roadstone and agricultural goods were charged at $1^1/_2$d. Payments due to the canal company were calculated with the aid of mileage posts which can still be seen today. An interesting leaflet on the canal is available from the Fourteen Locks Canal Centre at Rogerstone (Tel: 01633 894802).

Newport

Newport is so named to distinguish it from the earlier and older Roman port at Caerleon. A stone castle was built in 1191 to stand sentry over the river and it was not long before a town and trading centre developed. Enormous changes came when South Wales was industrialised in the 1750s. Up to that point the docks were no more than riverside wharfs but the opening of the canals from the valleys led to Newport becoming the principal coal port of the south. Along with the industrialisation came unrest and the town was the setting for the working-class Chartist riots in 1839 when John Frost, a distinguished citizen and one-time mayor, led a large demonstration. Many were shot and Frost

narrowly avoided hanging, being later transported. Perhaps the best known visual feature of Newport is the highly unusual Transporter Bridge which provides one of the routes for crossing the River Usk. There are only five other bridges of this type left in the world, with just two working examples left in Britain: here at Newport and Middlesbrough.

Tredegar House and Park

This was the home of one of the great Welsh families — the Morgans — for over 500 years until 1951. After this it was a school for 23 years and was acquired by Newport Borough for development as a recreational area. Guided tours lead you through both above-stairs and below-stairs rooms. The Morgans of Tredegar include many larger-than-life characters including Sir William who entertained Charles I, and other descendants who include a notorious pirate, a survivor of the Light Brigade, and a dabbler in black magic. The garden is open all year round and the house is open on certain days depending on the time of year (Tel: 01633 816069 for recorded information or 01633 815880 for other enquiries).

Starting Point: From the Riverway car park — see below.

Parking and Toilets: Park in the Riverway car park which as its name implies is alongside the River Usk on the west bank. This is a long-stay pay-and-display car park with reasonable charges. Toilets are available in nearby Newport town centre, which you can reach by the covered elevated walkway from the car park.

Distance: 6.6 miles (13.2 miles round trip).

Maps: Ordnance Survey Landranger Sheet 171.

Hills: Rather surprisingly for a canal ride, there is one steep climb due to the flight of 14 locks at Rogerstone.

Surface: The towpath is surfaced for most of its length and has a grit top dressing. On the whole the surface is good and may improve even more with the development of the Celtic Trail.

Left: Tredegar House. *Welsh Tourist Board*

ROUTE 17
THE MONMOUTHSHIRE & BRECON CANAL
Newport to the Prince of Wales
(Canalside Pub at Risca)

RISCA

River Usk

Fourteen Locks

Monmouthshire & Brecon Canal

M4

Castle

NEWPORT

Barrack Hill

Tredegar House Country Park

Safety: Care should be taken when cycling under the charming little canal bridges as their curved nature and narrowing of the towpath could lead to a nasty blow on the head or shoulder or a thorough wetting.

Roads and Road Crossings: The busy roads in Newport are avoided on this ride by the availability of subways and elevated walkways. There are number of road crossings due to the dismantling of parts of the canal over recent years to permit further road development. However, these are mostly minor but visibility is not good on some of them.

Refreshments: There is the Rising Sun and Olde Oak Inn at about $3^1/2$ miles outward ($9^1/2$ miles inward), and the Prince of Wales at the destination of the ride.

Nearest Tourist Information Centre: Museum and Art Gallery, John Frost Square, Newport NP9 1HZ (Tel: 01633 842962).

ROUTE INSTRUCTIONS

Getting to the canal at Barrack Hill from the Riverway car park is an intricate affair as you have to cross the busy main roads connecting Newport to the north and M4. Fortunately, subways and elevated walkways have been provided and the canal can be accessed without exposure to heavy traffic.

1. (0 miles): From the Riverway car park, follow the paved way past the Steel Wave sculpture towards the castle ruin. Pass under the road and rail bridges that cross the River Usk by dismounting and turning left into the subway tunnel, then right into another subway tunnel and then taking a 'wooden causeway' through the old castle ruin before continuing to follow the river bank. You will pass the side of Sainsbury's that most customers never see, and then go through some silver birch trees.

2. (0.8 miles): You will see a recreational park on the left, swing left here into a quiet residential street (Evans Street) and at the end, by the Old Rising Sun, dismount to cross Lyne Road to the pub side and continue along this road to the Spar Shop and Boilermakers' Club. Here turn left and pass the Coronation Working Men's Club. Pass under the elevated concrete roads to gain access to the elevated pedestrian crossing which you should use to cross the road and stream below safely.

3. (1.3 miles): The elevated crossing should deliver you to the start of the canal at Barrack Hill, where you should follow the towpath.

4. (2.0 miles): The canal forks here. You will need to take the spur to Pontywaun. This is the more obvious route and you should cycle over the steep ramp that enables you to cross the 'main' canal, to continue alongside the M4.

5. (3.0 miles): Cross under the M4.

6. (3.2 miles): At Bridge No 5, cross the canal to gain the towpath than now runs on the south side of the canal.

7. (3.4 miles) Cross the road just after the Fourteen Locks Centre — there is a convenience store here.

8. (3.6 miles) The towpath runs parallel to a road and close to the large Rising Sun Hotel and Restaurant.

9. (3.8 miles) Cross this busy road, with poor visibility by the Olde Oak.

10. (4.6 miles) Cross this fairly busy road; be careful as visibility is poor to the left.

11. (5.9 miles) Cross the road by Sue's General Store and Chip Shop.

12. (6.1 miles) Cross a quiet road.

13. (6.3 miles) Cross a further quiet road.

14. (6.6 miles) Arrive at the Prince of Wales. Be careful that you do not miss it, as it does not stand out as a pub from the towpath.

Left: Monmouth Canal Co mileage post.

THE MONMOUTHSHIRE & BRECON CANAL

GOYTRE WHARF TO LLANFOIST WHARF BY CANAL TOWPATH AND RETURN VIA THE USK VALLEY

'... lofty hills press on either banks of the widening but still impetuous river. A continuous chain of country seats, of glowing parklands and noble timber fill the narrow valley mile after mile or deck its lower slopes.'
Highways and Byways in South Wales by A. G. Bradley

You have two options on this ride. If you wish to remain completely off-road then you can cycle along the canal towpath from Goytre Wharf and back, which is a distance of about 12 miles. However, the circular route makes a more interesting ride where you cycle to Llanfoist Wharf and return via a B road to Llanellen, and then via very quiet country lanes in the Usk Valley to Croes Llanfair and finally back to Goytre Wharf. On the Saturday morning in June when I rode the route, I met only two cars and two farm vehicles on these lanes. The ride is described assuming that you are cycling the circular route. At the time of writing, this section of the towpath was not yet officially open to cyclists, but if you have a permit the authority will not object, although you will be cycling at your own risk. It is

important to remember that some of the towpath has a grass surface and therefore can be slippery when wet. Llanfoist is only 1 mile from Abergavenny, so if you have plenty of time then you could visit Abergavenny with its many attractions. This ride takes place on probably the most picturesque section of canal in the whole of Wales — made so by the nearby hills — Sugar Loaf Mountain ahead of you for most of the ride and Blorenge rising steeply from the canal and overshadowing it.

BACKGROUND AND PLACES OF INTEREST

The Monmouthshire & Brecon Canal

Although now called the Monmouthshire & Brecon Canal, the waterway from Newport to Brecon was built as two separate projects — the Brecon & Abergavenny Canal and the Monmouth Canal. The whole venture was finished in 1812 when the two canals were eventually linked. This waterway now stands as a self-contained feature but historically it has to be viewed with an associated complex tramroad network. While most canals in Wales were built for industrial purposes,

Below: Llanfoist Wharf.

mainly the transport of iron and coal to the seaports, the Brecon & Abergavenny was built to contribute to the agricultural economy. The majority of cargoes were farm produce, manure, lime and basic slag fertilizer. The coal that was carried was mainly for domestic use. The story of the closure of the canal is a familiar one. The 1850s saw the railway boom and many of the interconnecting tramroads were converted to railways. There was also some closure of ironworks that caused a decrease in the demand for limestone. The Great Western Railway Company took over the running of both canals in 1880 and, not really being interested, trade continued to slump. The last commercial traffic was carried in the 1930s. However, the canal is now restored for 33 miles from Brecon to Pontymoel (near Pontypool) and there are exciting plans to develop the whole corridor from Newport to Brecon.

Above: Which way now?

Abergavenny Museum and Castle
The remains of Abergavenny Castle lie to the southwest of Abergavenny. Only the motte and pentagonal bailey remain of the original building built by Hameline de Balun. The later stonework defences were included in the town walls and only the northwest wall and the ruins of the entrance gate and two mural towers still remain. At Christmas 1176, the castle was the scene of the notorious massacre of many of the Welsh lords of

Gwent by William de Braose, in revenge for the killing of his uncle by the Welsh. The museum is housed in an old hunting lodge within the castle grounds and presents the history of this market town from prehistoric and Roman times to the present. The two principal displays are a recreation of a Victorian Welsh farmhouse kitchen and a saddler's workshop. The museum is open every day in summer and is closed on Sundays in winter (Tel: 01873 854282 for more details).

Big Pit
Big Pit is a preserved coal mine that was in service from 1880 until 1980. On the surface you can guide yourself around a geographical background to the mine, the winding engine-house, a working blacksmith's yard and the old pithead baths. It is also possible to descend 300ft by cage, kitted with helmet and lamp and guided by an experienced miner, to view the old coal faces, underground workshops, stables and haulage engines. It should be noted that the underground tour is not suitable for children under 5 years of age. Any visitors in wheelchairs need to make prior arrangements to go underground. Open daily from March to November, 9.30am to 5pm, with the last tour beginning at 3.30pm (Tel: 01495 790311 for more information).

ROUTE 18
MONMOUTHSHIRE & BRECON CANAL
(Goytre Wharf to Llanfoist Wharf by Canal Towpath and return via the Usk Valley)

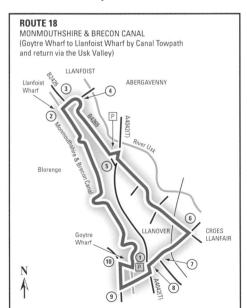

Starting Point: Goytre Wharf is the starting point for this ride. Going north from Pontypool on the A4042, take the turning into Saron Road signed 'Monmouth and Brecon Canal Goytre Wharf 1 mile'. You should note that the approach road to the wharf is closed nightly, between 7pm and 8.30am in the winter and between 10pm and 8.30am in the summer.

Parking and Toilets: There is a pay-and-display car park at the start of the ride at Goytre Wharf. There is also a car park at Llanellen.

Distance: 15 miles.

Maps: Ordnance Survey Landranger Sheet 161.

Hills: There are one or two short, sharp climbs on the country lanes between Llanellen and Croes Llanfair; otherwise the route is flat.

Surface: The surface of the towpath is, on the whole, good. It varies from a firm stony surface to grass, so it is best undertaken when the weather is not too wet. The grassy sections are occasionally rutted, so you need to be careful where you place your wheels.

Safety: Care should be taken when cycling under the charming little canal bridges as their curved nature and narrowing of the towpath could lead to a nasty blow on the head or shoulder or a thorough wetting.

Roads and Road Crossings: If you restrict the ride to the towpath there and back, there is no traffic to concern you. For the circular route, most of the on-road section is on quiet country lanes, However, about 2½ miles of the circular ride is on B roads that are fairly busy. There are also two crossings of the busy A4042(T) where care should be taken.

Refreshments: The Llanfoist Inn looks reasonably inviting. Alternatively there are several potential places for picnics along the towpath where two babbling brooks pass under the canal, or you might wish to stop on the return leg of the circular ride, close to the banks of the River Usk.

Nearest Tourist Information Centre: Swan Meadow, Monmouth Road, Abergavenny NP7 5HH (Tel: 01873 857588).

ROUTE INSTRUCTIONS

1. (0 miles): From the car park, cycle under the aqueduct (by Aqueduct Cottage) and then turn immediately left to climb up to the towpath by the steep path.

2. (5.7 miles): At Llanfoist Wharf, descend the steps with your cycle to join a tarmac lane where you should cycle down past the church, possibly accompanied (dependent upon the season), by a babbling brook.

3. (5.9 miles): At the junction with the B4246 turn right you will pass the Llanfoist Inn.

4. (6.2 miles): Turn right where signposted to Llanellen on the B4269.

5. (8.3 miles): Turn left on the road that passes the village hall to cut through to the A4042. Carefully cross the A4042 to take the narrow country lane almost opposite.

6. (11.2 miles): At the crossroads, turn right as indicated to 'Goytre 1½ Nant-y-derry 1¾'.

7. (12.4 miles): At the junction with the road to Nant-y-derry, go straight on as signposted to Pontypool and Abergavenny.

8. (12.7 miles): At the junction with the A4042, turn left (there is a pavement here to keep you safe) and after a short distance, carefully cross the road into Saron Road which is signposted back to 'Goytre Wharf 1 mile'.

9. (13.8 miles): Turn right at the junction by Ty-Cooke Farm which is, confusingly, again signposted 'Goytre Wharf 1 mile'.

10. (14.7 miles): Turn right at the entrance to Goytre Wharf.

1. (15.0 miles): Arrive back at the Goytre Wharf car park.

Below: The start of the ride at Goytre Wharf.

THE SIRHOWY VALLEY RAILPATH
FULL MOON VISITOR CENTRE TO THE HALFWAY HOUSE PUB AT WYLLIE

'Beneath these towns, if you take the trouble to find it, is the beauty of pride and endurance. The beauty of North Wales is the beauty of hill lying against hill, the coming of dawn and the fall of the mists at night. But in the south you have woman struggling to keep her home together and man hoping against hope that the tide will turn.' H. V. Morton from *In Search of Wales*

This route forms part of the Newport to Blackwood Cycleway and takes you along a disused railway line that replaced the former Sirhowy Tramroad built in 1805 to carry pig iron and coal from Tredegar to Newport on horse-drawn trams. The line follows the wooded Sirhowy River Valley and streams gush forth from the hill above you and drain into the river below. The countryside hereabouts, although heavily moulded by man, has managed to retain its inherent beauty. Glimpses of the characteristic hillside terraced housing of these valleys frequently appear between gaps in the trees. It is a pleasant secluded and quiet ride and we met only two other cyclists during the afternoon spent surveying the route. We did meet lots of school children who were doing some field work and having a marvellous time. The route forms an important part of the South Wales Cycleway, also known as the Celtic Trail which is planned to run from Newport to Kidwelly. This will be built to National Cycle Network standards and will become Route 4 of the National Network.

BACKGROUND AND PLACES OF INTEREST

The Sirhowy Valley Country Park
This is one of the newest and largest country parks in Wales, amounting to a total of 760 acres. There is the Full Moon Visitor Centre (open in summer only, Tel: 01495 270991), picnic sites, fitness and orienteering routes. In addition to the visitor centre there is the Ynys

Above: The Sirhowy Valley.

Hywel Countryside Centre which has been developed from a Welsh long house built in 1776. Here you can obtain refreshments in the afternoon, only a few minutes away from the cycle route. (Tel: 01495 200113 to check whether it is open, as this varies seasonally.)

Cwmcarn Forest Drive
This is a 7-mile motoring route within the 1,000-acre Ebbw Forest and follows a high forest road with several places to stop and picnic. There is an adventure playground and superb views across the Severn Estuary. Twmbarlwm hillfort shows evidence of human existence in these parts from a Bronze Age burial site through an Iron Age hillfort to a Roman signal station, which later became a Norman motte. From here you can see every type of feature that makes up this part of South Wales. Narrow towns along valley bottoms, grassed-over coaltips, conifers, farmland and of course sheep. Further afield there are the docks of Newport, the capital city of Cardiff and finally the sea with the islands of Flatholm and Steepholm. There is a small visitor centre and shop (Tel: 01495 272001 for more information).

Gelligroes Mill
This is a 17th-century water-powered, stone-built grain mill. It has been restored to full working condition and it is here that a young radio amateur listened to the last messages from the stricken liner *Titanic* and Islwyn, the famous Welsh Bard, learned the traditional metre. There are history and technology displays and a candle workshop nearby with many unusual designs (Tel: 01495 222053 for more information).

Starting Point: From the small lay-by car park at the entrance to the country park.

Parking and Toilets: It may be better for you to park in the small lay-by car park outside the barrier at the entrance to the country park, rather than the 'inside' car park. This avoids the danger of your car becoming locked in, as the barrier is locked in the late afternoon. There are toilets at the Full Moon Visitor Centre and at the Ynys Hywel Centre during opening hours.

Distance: 4.3 miles (8.6 miles there and back).

Maps: Ordnance Survey Landranger Sheet 171.

Hills: None.

Surface: Very good gritted surface often wide enough for two bikes side by side.

Safety: This is a very easy and safe route suitable for all members of the family.

Roads and Road Crossings: Two crossings of very minor roads and a short distance on a quiet lane to get to the pub at the end of the ride.

Refreshments: The Ynys Hywel Centre has refreshments available in the afternoons at weekends and Bank Holidays. The Halfway House pub at the end of the ride advertises 'excellent food'. There are also many attractive picnic sites available throughout the park.

Nearest Tourist Information Centre: Lower Twyn Square, Caerphilly, CF83 1XX (Tel: 01222 880011).

ROUTE INSTRUCTIONS

Virtually no directions are required on this very straightforward ride — it is one of the easiest in the book.

1. (0 miles): Take the surfaced drive past the Full Moon Visitor Centre.

2. (0.5 miles): The cycle route veers away from the car park through a green barrier.

3. (1.5 miles): Cross a very quiet road.

4. (4.2 miles): At the end of the cycleway, carry on along a drive with two concrete strips.

5. (4.3 miles): Cross the quiet Heolddu Road to finish the ride at the Halfway House pub.

Below left: The beautiful Sirhowy River.

Below: The railpath is wide enough for two.

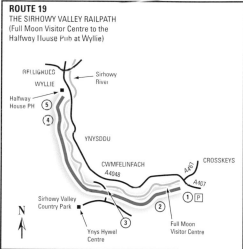

ROUTE 19
THE SIRHOWY VALLEY RAILPATH
(Full Moon Visitor Centre to the Halfway House Pub at Wyllie)

THE TAFF TRAIL
CARDIFF TO TONGWYNLAIS

'Cardiff is a beautiful and dignified city. One feels on seeing it for the first time as one feels when meeting some congenial and charming person of whom one has heard nothing but slander...' H. V. Morton from *In Search of Wales*

The Taff Trail has enormous scope for quiet cycling. It is a long-distance trail running from Cardiff Docks in the south to Brecon in the north. Almost all of it is traffic-free with some short sections on mostly quiet roads. It is so called because for a large part of its length it runs parallel with the River Taff through the Taff Valley. Also running through the valley is the Merthyr Tydfil to Cardiff railway line. This has many small stations and provides the added benefit of allowing you to cycle from perhaps Cardiff to Pontypridd or Merthyr Tydfil and to return by rail without retracing your route. The four rides in this book concentrate on the traffic-free sections. This one takes us from the noise and bustle of the capital city, enjoying some very attractive riverside scenes and views of Llandaff Cathedral, to within sight of the 'fairytale castle' of Castell Coch.

BACKGROUND AND PLACES OF INTEREST

Cardiff
The capital city of Wales has a population of 290,000 and is a very elegant city and port. It was born of the Industrial Revolution, its population increasing from 1,000 in 1801 to over 180,000 in 1911. The spacious central part of the city is striking with its impressive castle, its riverside parks — some of which you pass through on this ride — and its pleasant pedestrian precincts. The southern half of the city has recently been transformed by Europe's most exciting waterfront development — the Cardiff Bay Development Project. Its basic aim is to revitalise the city's industrial heart and include commerce, the professions, housing, recreation and culture. A large city always has plenty to see and do. The city area has Cardiff Castle (Tel: 01222 822083) which is situated on the site of a Roman fortress and a medieval stronghold. Like many features that you will see on the Taff Trail, the present castle was created by one of the Bute family — the third Marquis of Bute. The city centre also contains the National Museum of Wales (Tel: 01222 397951) and many other attractions. The dock area has the Welsh Industrial and Maritime Museum (Tel: 01222 481919) which has a replica of Trevithick's steam engine that first

Below: Cardiff Castle. *Welsh Tourist Board*

Above: Llandaff Weir.

ran on the tramroad from Abercynon to Merthyr Tydfil — the tramroad forms part of Route 22. Other attractions are the Cardiff Bay Visitor Centre (Tel: 01222 463833) and Techniquest (Tel: 01222 475475) with its 'hands on' science and technology exhibits.

Llandaff Cathedral
A small diversion from the trail (see directions) will take you to the historic city of Llandaff — in reality part of Cardiff — and its magnificent cathedral. Llandaff is one of those minute 'cities' for which Wales is famous. St Asaph and St David's are 'city' villages and I suppose that you would call Llandaff a 'city' suburb. It has been restored twice; the first work was done in 1869 and a major restoration was also carried out in 1957 to repair serious war damage. It is sited on one of the oldest religious sites in Great Britain which was first used in the ninth century. The restored Bishop's Palace is situated close by and was located to guard the river ford.

Mellingriffith Water Pump
Situated by the trail just north of Llandaff, this is believed locally to be one of the most important industrial monuments in Europe. It dates from 1807 and is a water-powered beam engine whose purpose was to lift water from the feeder of the Mellingriffith Tin Plate Works to the Glamorganshire Canal, which is now filled in. The pump is driven by an undershot waterwheel and worked for 140 years lifting water 11ft up into the canal. These canal pumps always impress me with the elegance of their design — carrying out their function over such a long period without consuming any fuel whatsoever.

Starting Point: This ride starts from Cardiff Central railway station which is only a few hundred yards from the trail.

Parking and Toilets: I parked in the railway station pay-and-display car park. There are many other car parks in central Cardiff. There are toilets in Tongwynlais.

Distance: This is a linear ride of 6 miles (12 miles there and back). With the aid of the Cardiff to Merthyr Tydfil railway service (operated by Valley Lines) it is possible to cycle just the 6 miles and make your way to Radyr or Taff's Well stations and return by train to Cardiff Central. Alternatively, it is possible to lengthen your ride by increments and return from one of several other stations. Thirteen stations are accessible over the full length of the trail and a limited number of cycles can be carried free at off-peak times. For information on train services and fares telephone 01222 231978.

Maps: Ordnance Survey Landranger Sheet 171.

Hills: Easy grading, with no significant hills. If you carry on to Castle Coch there is a steep climb between the village of Tongwynlais and the castle.

Surface: A mixture of gravelled tracks and tarmac surface.

Safety: Care is necessary when joining the route, negotiating road crossings and when cycling through Tongwynlais.

Roads and Road Crossings: It is necessary to negotiate some busy routes at the start of the ride for about 0.2 mile. Castle Street and Western Avenue (by a subway) are crossed. There are a couple of very short sections where the trail follows quiet drives with limited vehicular access and a short stretch of road of about 0.2 miles in Tongwynlais.

Refreshments: In Tongwynlais there is the Old Ton Inn and the Lewis Arms. We refreshed ourselves at the Lewis Arms which was very pleasant. There are a couple of tables outside where we watched the world go by on a sunny April afternoon for an hour or so.

Nearest Tourist Information Centre: Cardiff Central Station, Central Square, Cardiff CF1 1QY (Tel: 01222 227281).

Further Information: There is a cycle shop in Tongwynlais. The official guidebook to the trail and a series of 6 free leaflets is obtainable from the Taff Trail Project which is based in Aberdare (Tel: 01685 883880).

ROUTE INSTRUCTIONS

The route is exceptionally well waymarked by the Taff Trail 'Viaduct' logo and the National Cycle Route signs, so on the whole directions are not necessary. Instructions are given only if the route deviates from the trail, or if the waymarking does not make the route to take absolutely clear.

1. (0 miles): With the station behind you, turn left. (This short section that takes us to join the Taff Trail is on busy roads, so you may wish to walk if you have young children.) Turn left at the traffic lights (Wood Street) and cross the river via the bridge to join the Taff Trail on the west bank of the river.

2. (0.5 miles): At the Castle Street Bridge cross the dual carriageway and rejoin the trail.

3. (2.0 miles): After passing through the parkland of Llandaff Fields the drive meets Western Avenue. Turn right here and avoid crossing the road by walking along the right-hand side of the bridge and then passing down the steps to gain access to the opposite river bank and resume your course up-river by using the small subway. (If you wish to detour into Llandaff you should turn left here and right into Cardiff Road.)

4. (5.8 miles): Where Iron Bridge Road meets a main road, turn left. You are now on a road for the short distance into Tongwynlais.

5. (6.0 miles): Arrive in Tongwynlais.

Below: The Norwegian church, Cardiff Bay. *Welsh Tourist Board*

ROUTE 20
THE TAFF TRAIL
(Cardiff to Tongwynlais)

TONGWYNLAIS
5
4
M4 Motorway
RADYR
P The Mellingriffith Water Pump
LLANDAFF NORTH
River Taff
LLANDAFF 3
CARDIFF CITY CENTRE
N
2
P 1 CARDIFF CENTRAL STATION

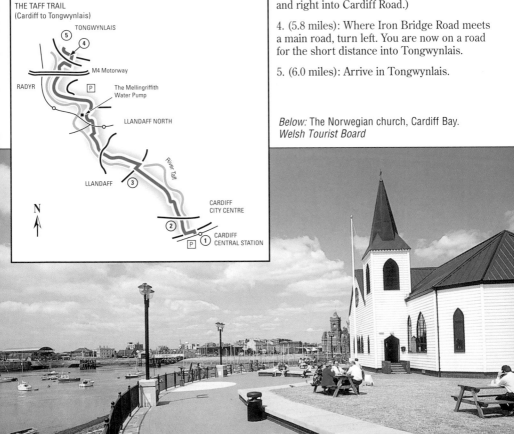

THE TAFF TRAIL
CASTELL COCH TO PONTYPRIDD

'I hope some people will take my advice. These mining valleys do not want compassion or charity. But they are worth understanding; and they are friendly, and their beauty is not that of sun or moon, but of the human heart.' H. V. Morton writing in the 1930s about the depressed mining valleys of the area in his *In Search of Wales*

This part of the Taff Trail takes us from Castell Coch, which is one of the most fascinating surviving examples of Victorian medievalism, to the market town of Pontypridd. After the climb above Castell Coch, the route is mostly elevated with fine views across the Taff Valley and towards Cardiff from the viewing platform at the halfway point. Parts of the route follow the old Barry and Rhymney railway lines. The route is well used by the local population for recreation at weekends and everyone that you pass seems to find time to have a pleasant word to say.

Above: Castell Coch — the 'fairytale castle' designed by the 19th-century architect William Burges. *Welsh Tourist Board*

BACKGROUND AND PLACES OF INTEREST

Castell Coch
The 'fairytale castle' looks as if it should have been built in Bavaria rather than Wales. It is an eye-catching landmark and was designed in the 1870s by William Burges for the third Marquis of Bute, although it stands on the site of a much earlier medieval fortification. It is now a Grade 1 listed building. The interior is especially magnificent, particularly the octagonal Drawing Room which is decorated with plants, birds and carved butterflies. It is open daily throughout the year and there is an admission charge. (Tel: 01222 810101 for more information.)

Taff's Well
Having been born in Bath and now living there again, it is not surprising that spas interest me. There is something very pleasant about the notion of taking the waters rather than drugs to improve your health. In the

19th century, the warm waters made it a popular, if small, healing resort. The well produced water similar in analysis to that of Bath, although cooler, with a pea-green colour and with its surface broken with the rise of nitrogen and carbonic acid gas. The village also has links with St David, the patron saint of Wales.

Pontypridd

Pontypridd is a market town, not without interest. It has a very distinctive and elegant single arch bridge which was built in 1756 and it took three attempts before it would stand up. Although it has an attractive shape, it is too steep for wheeled traffic. There is a splendid park — Ynysangharad War Memorial Park — where there is a sculpture that commemorates the composers of the Welsh National Anthem. The traffic-free section of the ride ends at Glyntaff Crematorium, which is appropriate as the origin of legal cremation can be found in the town. A Dr William Price, a mystic and Druid, was arrested in 1884 for cremating his infant son. After a famous court case, cremation was eventually legalised in this country.

Starting Point: This ride starts from Castell Coch.

Parking and Toilets: Good parking facilities are available at Castell Coch. Please note that there are no toilets at Castell Coch.

Distance: 6.9 miles (13.8 miles there and back).

Maps: Ordnance Survey Landranger Sheets 170 and 171.

Hills: There is one extremely steep hill at the beginning where the route climbs through Fforest-fawr — a beautiful beech woodland above Castell Coch. There is no alternative other than to walk it — and legally you are required to do so anyway — but do not be put off as the rest of the route is essentially cycleable.

Surface: Very good, often stone-based with a gritty top dressing.

Below: Pontypridd Bridge — too steep for wheeled traffic.

Opposite page: The River Taff at Pontypridd.

Safety: There are no particular hazards associated with this ride except the road crossings highlighted below.

Roads and Road Crossings: There is a crossing of the very busy A468 Taff Valley to Caerphilly road. This is a dual carriageway so it is possible to cross it in reasonable safety in two halves. Otherwise there is only very limited on-road cycling apart from the approach into Pontypridd from the Glyntaff Crematorium, which shares main roads for short distances.

Refreshments: My advice is to take a picnic as there is very little opportunity for refreshment other than at the end of the ride in Pontypridd.

Nearest Tourist Information Centre: Bridge Street, Pontypridd CF37 4PE (Tel: 01443 409512).

ROUTE INSTRUCTIONS

The route is exceptionally well waymarked by the Taff Trail 'Viaduct' logo, brown cycle route signboards and National Cycle Route signs, so on the whole directions are not necessary. Instructions are given only if the route deviates from the trail, or if the waymarking does not make the route absolutely clear.

1. (0 miles): With Castell Coch behind you, walk the steep hill up through the woods.

2. (0.2 miles): At the top of the steep climb from Castell Coch you have a choice of routes; turn left and start cycling!

3. (0.7 miles): Look out for two white posts on the left and turn here (if you miss these and descend to go under the bridge you will leave the Taff Trail).

4. (2.1 miles): After crossing under the 'sloping' road bridge, it is important that you take the left-hand route that climbs a short 'hairpin' hill which brings you to the A468 Caerphilly road at Nantgarw.

5. (2.2 miles): At the junction with the A468 — close to the huge GEAES site — use the pedestrian crossing to cross this busy road. You will see a sign between the carriageways 'Pontypridd 5 miles' — this is the direction you need to follow. On this part of the ride there are no Taff Trail signs, so you will need

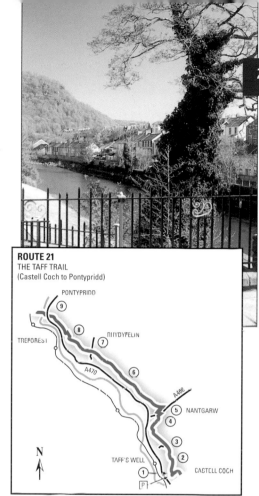

ROUTE 21
THE TAFF TRAIL
(Castell Coch to Pontypridd)

to follow the brown cycleway signs and Welsh National Cycle Route signs. Cycle through a housing estate on quiet roads and you will find that the Taff Trail re-establishes its route.

6. (3.4 miles): You will see the Treforest Industrial Estate down on your left.

7. (4.5 miles): Cross a quiet road to pass through an extensive council housing estate at Rhydyfelin.

8. (5.9 miles): The traffic-free part of the ride ends at the Glyntaff Crematorium. From here your route into Pontypridd is via Pentrebach Road and Ynysangharad Road. A very busy roundabout takes you into Bridge Street and over the River Taff into Pontypridd.

9. (6.9 miles): Arrive in Pontypridd.

THE TAFF TRAIL
PONTYPRIDD TO MERTHYR TYDFIL

'On I wandered. After some time the valley assumed the form of an immense basin...Down below meandered the Taf, its reaches shining with a silver-like splendour. The whole together formed an exquisite picture, in which there was much sublimity, much still quiet life, and not a little of fantastic fairy loveliness.' George Borrow from his *Wild Wales* as he was tramping from Merthyr Tydfil to Quakers Yard

Although never very far from settlements, this ride spends a considerable time submerged in the beautiful Taff Valley hidden from most of human life. The route uses the disused communications from the valley's industrial past — canal towpaths and tramroads — that were used to transport the materials from Merthyr's iron and coal industry to Cardiff. This valley, like the others that spread out like fingers from Cardiff northwestward, is now clean and quiet. The slag heaps and spoil heaps are now greening over, to the point where it is now difficult to tell hill from heap. This route is mainly traffic-free with a limited amount of road use. Again

you can take advantage of the Cardiff to Merthyr Tydfil railway and cycle from Pontypridd to Merthyr or one of the other stations in between and bring your bikes back on the train, but avoid peak times. (Tel: 01222 430460 for more information.)

BACKGROUND AND PLACES OF INTEREST

Merthyr Tydfil
The name means Tydfil's burial place, with the first word being the Welsh for martyr and therefore signifying the place where the martyr was buried. Merthyr is central to the story of the coal, iron and steel industries of Wales. It was the 18th century that brought the massive industrial build up, with the opening of John Guest's Dowlais Ironworks in 1759, followed quickly by Crawshay's at Cyfarthfa in 1765, Hill's Plymouth Works in 1767 and Hamfray's at Pen-y-Darren in 1784. In 1831, the population was greater than that of Cardiff, Swansea and Newport combined. On this ride, as you approach Merthyr from Pontypridd you will see many relics of the industrial past. The Glamorganshire Canal was a major step forward as it replaced slow pack horses with water transport. In turn the many locks on the canal between Merthyr and Abercynon were a deterrent to use and the Pen-y-Darren Horse Tramroad was opened to bypass these. Finally Brunel's railway to Cardiff was opened in 1841 and this is the current Valley Line. Although in those days Merthyr was commercially prosperous, it was for most people a grim and smoky collection of ugly iron and coal workings which had one of the worst public health records in Britain.

Cyfarthfa Castle
This stands in a large hillside park of 160 acres and was built in an ostentatious castellated style in 1825, enabling its owner William Crawshaw to survey his nearby ironworks. It was sold in 1909 to the Merthyr Corporation and was converted to a museum and school. It is now a Grade 1 listed building and houses the borough's distinguished museum and art gallery (Tel: 01685 723112 for information).

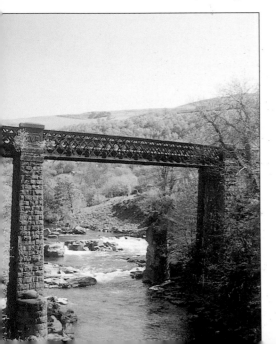

Left: The River Taff north of Pontypridd.

Left: Aberfan Cemetery.

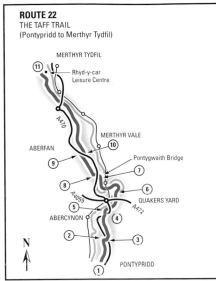

ROUTE 22
THE TAFF TRAIL
(Pontypridd to Merthyr Tydfil)

Quakers Yard

The ride passes through this small settlement which is so named after the Quaker burial ground that was opened in 1667 and used as a meeting place and graveyard until 1891. George Borrow visited here on a walk from Merthyr Tydfil to Caerphilly when writing *Wild Wales* (1862). His forthright nature led to an argument with a local resident who had an unfounded dislike for Quakers. A lively encounter ensued and he advised the man not to speak ill of people of whom he was ignorant. He described Quakers Yard thus: 'A lovely resting place looked that little oblong yard on the peninsula, by the confluence of the waters, and quite in keeping with the character of the quiet Christian people who sleep within it.' These days (or at least on my visit) the enclosure was an untidy mess, full of broken bottles, beer cans and litter. A disgrace would be the best word for it — I just hope that tidying up does occur on a regular basis and my visit was just before the next regular clean-up.

Aberfan Cemetery and the nearby Memorial Gardens

If you ask people of around my age to name the events they can remember from the 1960s, the Aberfan disaster usually comes a close second to President Kennedy's assassination. The slipping of the coal tips crushed many houses and the village school and over 100 children were tragically killed. The Aberfan Cemetery lies alongside the trail and it is difficult not to be touched emotionally as you gaze at the sight of those two long rows of arched memorial stones, representing such a huge loss of young lives.

Pen-y-Darren Tramroad

Part of the route follows this old tramroad. It is preserved as a scheduled ancient monument and is where in 1804 the first ever steam locomotive railway journey took place, powered by Richard Trevithick's engine.

Starting Point: Where the traffic-free section resumes at Coedpenmaen Road in Pontypridd.

Parking and Toilets: I parked at the Sardis Road car park which has the advantage of being free, but it is on the far side of town from the start of the traffic-free section of the trail. The town centre car park is closer but very expensive. You need to be careful with some of these Pontypridd car parks as they lock them up in the evening (7pm in the case of Sardis Road).

Distance: 13 miles (26 miles there and back). With the aid of the Cardiff to Merthyr Tydfil railway service (operated by Valley Lines) it is possible to cycle just the 13 miles, make your way to Merthyr Tydfil station and return by train to Pontypridd. Alternatively, it is possible to shorten your ride by returning via one of the four intervening stations. A limited number of cycles can be carried free at off-peak times. For information on train services and fares telephone 01222 430460.

Maps: Ordnance Survey Landranger Sheets 160, 170 and 171 (very small part of route).

Hills: There is only one significant climb — between the subways at Buarth Glas and Merthyr Vale.

Surface: Very good, except the stretch that follows the Pen-y-Darren Tramroad where the original trackbed and stone sleepers remain.

Safety: Be careful on the old Pen-y-Darren Tramroad (see above).

Roads and Road Crossings: There is about a mile on a major road (the A4054 into Abercynon), but this is fairly quiet as through traffic takes the parallel trunk route. There is the occasional short length on quiet lanes.

Refreshments: My advice is to take a picnic as there is very little opportunity for refreshment other than at the end of the ride.

Nearest Tourist Information Centre: Bridge Street, Pontypridd CF37 4PE (Tel: 01443 409512).

ROUTE INSTRUCTIONS

Although on-street parking is possible in Coedpenmaen Road at the start of the ride, it is more considerate to use a designated car park. Assuming that you use one of the town car parks the following directions to the start of the route (from Bridge Street) may be helpful:

■ From Bridge Street facing east, turn left into West Street.
■ Keep following this one-way street until you come to the crossroads marked by the Central Hotel.
■ Straight on here to pass Trallwng Infants School.
■ Enter Bonvilston Road (ignore the Taff Trail sign directing you left, which is intended to take travellers in the opposite direction into Pontypridd).
■ At the junction where Bonvilston Road meets Coedpenmaen Road, turn left

Left: Waymarker at Abercanaid.

and you will see the Taff Trail sign (Abercynon 2³/₄ miles) at the end of the road.

The route is exceptionally well waymarked by the Taff Trail 'Viaduct' logo, brown cycle route signboards and National Cycle Route signs, so directions are not generally necessary. Instructions are given only if the route deviates from the trail, or if the waymarking does not make the route absolutely clear.

1. (0 miles): At the end of Coedpenmaen Road — there is a terrace of houses on the left called Lower Taff View — descend the tarmac slope to pick up the route on the river bank.

2. (1.0 miles): Emerge from the trail and turn right (east).

3. (1.2 miles): By Coedylan School swing left and after a short distance cross the bridge over the A470(T) to turn left onto the A4054 that runs parallel with the trunk road.

4. (2.6 miles): Turn left at the traffic lights to cross back over the A470(T) and then swing right into Abercynon.

5. (2.9 miles): At the fire station turn right into a quieter road.

6. (4.1 miles): Cross Goitrecoed Road at Quakers Yard.

7. (5.9 miles): The trail meets a narrow lane where you turn left to pass Pontygwaith Farm and cross the River Taff via Pontygwaith Bridge.

8. (6.1 miles): Cross to the east side of the A470(T) to gain access to a quiet lane, using the Buarth Glas subway.

9. (7.6 miles): A second subway will take you back under the A470(T).

10. (7.8 miles): Very soon after the subway turn sharp left (this is easy to miss as you speed downhill).

11. (12.6 miles): The ride ends by the Rhyd-y-car Leisure Centre. If you wish to return to Pontypridd by train using Merthyr railway station, cross the River Taff via the road bridge, follow the road until you pass under the railway viaduct and turn left for the station.

THE TAFF TRAIL
MERTHYR TYDFIL TO
TALYBONT-ON-USK

'As a viewpoint the Beacons are superb: given that rare right day you see to Cadair Idris in the north and away to Exmoor in the south.'
William Condry writing in *Exploring Wales*

This is the fourth section of the Taff Trail that I have explored and without doubt it is the best. We leave the valleys along the route of the old railway line which at one time ran from Merthyr to Brecon and gradually climb up into the Brecon Beacons National Park. The route passes the blue-black waters of Ponsticill and Pentwyn Reservoirs and through the Taf Fechan Forest to the high point of the ride at 439m near the beautiful waterfalls at Blaen-y-glyn. There is then a long gentle descent following the old railway trackbed to Aber village, during which there are superb views looking down onto the Talybont Reservoir. From here it is only a short stretch via a country road into Talybont. A truly memorable ride.

Suggested Sections For Less Experienced Cyclists
This is a long and demanding ride; some of it is suitable for almost all cyclists — the first section on the old railway track out of Merthyr for example — but there are steep gradients and about 6 miles of the 17½ miles are on roads that are basically quiet but can be busy in the main holiday season or on Bank Holidays. Here are a couple of suggestions for easy rides that concentrate on the traffic-free sections, avoid the more difficult terrain, and are therefore suitable for families with children:
■ Park at the start of the ride at Point 1 and ride to the end of the first railway section at Point 2 to enjoy the Taf Fechan Nature Reserve and dramatic limestone gorges (5.2 miles there and back).

■ Park at the high point of the ride at Point 11 and follow the old section of railway line high above the river valley that feeds the Talybont Reservoir and descends slowly to skirt the edge of the reservoir to Point 12. You could then use the road (which is quiet) around the other side of the reservoir to return to your starting place. There is the problem of a short stiff climb at the very end. Families should arrange to end their ride by the bridge that crosses the river and send dad or mum back to walk the steep ½ mile to fetch the car! (10 mile circular route).

BACKGROUND AND PLACES OF INTEREST

Talybont-on-Usk
The name of this pleasant hamlet is not entirely correct as it does not lie exactly on the Usk. However, it is situated firmly on another watercourse — the beautiful Monmouthshire & Brecon Canal. While the Usk flows in a broad and attractive valley about ½ mile from the centre of Talybont, the canal has been excavated from a shoulder of land above the village.

Below: Pontsarn Viaduct.

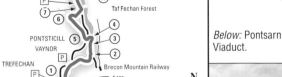

ROUTE 23
THE TAFF TRAIL
(Merthyr Tydfil to Talybont-on-Usk)

TALYBONT-ON-USK
⑭ Star Inn
⑬ ⑫ White Hart Inn
P Blaen-y-glyn
⑨ ⑪
Talybont Forest
⑧ ⑩
P Taf Fechan Forest
⑦ ⑥
④
PONTSTICILL ⑤ ③
VAYNOR P ②
TREFECHAN
P ① Brecon Mountain Railway
A465
Heads of the Valleys Rd
MERTHYR TYDFIL

N

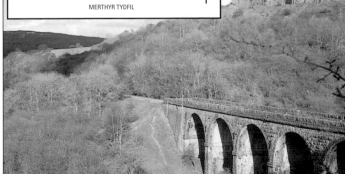

It is a beautiful meandering canal that is a treasured and most valuable recreational facility. It seems to pop up unexpectedly wherever you are driving in the area. Construction of the canal was begun in 1797 and was opened on Christmas Eve in 1800 — a considerable feat in itself. It was the main transport route in the area, and horse-drawn boats were used to carry coal, limestone, woollen and leather goods, agricultural produce and beer. With the arrival of the steam railway, the canal fell into decline and it closed in the 1930s and lay neglected for a while. Fortunately, British Waterways and the National Park authorities worked together to restore the canal and it was reopened in 1970.

Brecon Beacons National Park
The Brecon Beacons National Park covers, in my opinion, 520 square miles of some of the most beautiful scenery in Britain. I like my hills and mountains to be feminine and attractive, not craggy and masculine and it is their rounded form that makes them so pleasing to me. Nevertheless, the two chief summits — Pen y Fan and Corn Ddu reach a height of 2,907ft and 2,863ft respectively and when I cycled here in April, these sandstone peaks still had a significant covering of snow. One look at the Ordnance Survey map soon confirms that this is some of the finest walking country in Britain, with the area criss-crossed with rights of way through valleys and over mountain tops. The National Park Mountain Centre (named after Sir Brian Mountain) is open daily on the upland Mynydd Illtyd Common about 6 miles from Brecon (Tel: 01874 623366).

Brecon Mountain Railway
The route passes very close to the railway and if you are a railway enthusiast you may very well wish to take a ride. It is a narrow gauge line that follows the route of the old Brecon & Merthyr Railway (1859-1962) and runs for two miles into the Brecon Beacons alongside the Pontsticill Reservoir. The main station is Pant station, Dowlais, about 3 miles north of Merthyr Tydfil and there is also a stop near Pontsticill. Close to the main station there is an interesting workshop where small engines are restored to work on the line. A ride on the railway is an excellent opportunity to observe the countryside at leisure. (Generally open April-October daily, Tel: 01685 722988.)

Above: Mountain bikers near Pontsticill Reservoir.

Starting Point: From the lay-by in Vaynor Road.

Parking and Toilets: I parked in the large lay-by in Vaynor Road which is marked as a car park for Taf Fechan and Gilsanws Nature Reserves. It is about 1/2 mile from the junction of Vaynor Road and the High Street. Parking is also possible near the Pontsarn Inn for a reasonable charge, and there are several opportunities for free car parking along the route in the Brecon Beacons National Park.

Distance: 17.5 miles (35 miles there and back). For families with young children, see earlier suggestions for short rides from car parks along the route.

Maps: Ordnance Survey Landranger Sheets 160 and 161.

Hills: The ride starts with little gradient, but as the trail makes its way through Taf Fechan Forest the route becomes very steep and use of a mountain bike would be preferable.

Surface: Varied, but mostly good, consisting of old railway trackbeds, forest tracks and some on-road sections. The surface can be a little rough on the off-road climb through Taf Fechan Forest.

Safety: There are no particular hazards on this ride.

Roads and Road Crossings: A significant element of this section of the Taff Trail is on minor country roads that are not fast but can become busy in the holiday season.

Refreshments: There are two interesting-looking inns a mile or so from the beginning of the ride — the Pontsarn Inn and the Aberglais Inn. There are two pubs in Pontsticill and several in Talybont, one of which — the Star — is renowned for its ales and ciders. It is important to note that there are no sources of refreshment between Pontsticill and Talybont, so if you are doing the whole ride then I would advise that a picnic should be taken, with a view to stopping possibly by a mountain stream at the highest point of the ride.

Nearest Tourist Information Centre: 14a Glebeland Street, Merthyr Tydfil CF47 8AU (Tel: 01685 379884).

ROUTE INSTRUCTIONS

1. (0 miles): From the car park, cross the road as directed to the Taf Fechan Nature Reserve, pass under the steel restriction bar and climb down the steps to join the Taff Trail.

2. (2.6 miles): Leave the old railway line by the small waterfall and steps to take the road for a short distance.

3. (3.1 miles): Bear right to take the higher of the two lanes (this junction is very close to the river).

4. (3.5 miles): Swing left to take the road across the top of the Pontsticill Reservoir dam, swing left toward Pontsticill and then after a short distance take the acute right turn — signposted 'Talybont on Usk 2½'.

5. (4.3 miles): Turn left off the road and take the forest track.

6. (5.8 miles): Between two boulders strike off down the tarmac slope to cross an attractive wooden bridge.

7. (6.6 miles): The track meets the road and you should turn left, and almost immediately you will need to swing left as directed to 'Talybont on Usk 8½'.

8. (7.8 miles): Do not turn off sharp right down the hill, but take the very quiet lane that goes straight on.

9. (9.1 miles): Take an acute right turn off the lane onto a track which takes you through fields and several gates.

10. (10.2 miles): Join the road again, turn left and continue on the stiff climb toward the highest point of the ride.

11. (10.7 miles): Turn off right through the green metal barrier to join the old Brecon & Merthyr Railway track.

12. (15.7 miles): Swing left to cross the Talybont Reservoir dam wall.

13. (16.0 miles): At the end of the dam wall turn right and take the road to Talybont-on-Usk.

14. (17.5 miles): Arrive at the intriguing swing bridge across the Monmouthshire & Brecon Canal in Talybont-on-Usk.

Below: The swing bridge on the canal near Talybont.

🚲 ROUTE 24

AFAN FOREST PARK
A DELIGHTFUL RIDE ALONG BOTH SIDES OF THE AFAN VALLEY

'An iron bridge crossed the valley and over it go coal wagons…Black paths, beaten hard as ebony by the feet of generations, lead steeply from the rows of grey houses to the presiding deity of all Glamorganshire vales — the colliery.' H. V. Morton writing in the 1930s about the mining valleys of South Wales in his *In Search of Wales*

The geography and industrial history of the now beautiful Afan Valley combine together to provide a wonderful opportunity for a traffic-free ride up and down the valley on either side of the River Afan. The outward leg from the Afan Argoed Countryside Centre follows the route of the old Rhondda & Swansea Bay Railway line on the south side of the valley. This route follows the line as far as Cymer and then crosses the river and returns on its north side. However, from here it is possible to extend the ride by a further 4¹/₂ miles (return journey) on a traffic-free path to Glyncorrwg. The ride then returns on the north side of the valley to cross back over the river via a small footbridge. However, a further extension is possible here. If you avoid crossing back over the river and carry on to Pontrhydyfen you can come from Pontrhydyfen on the south side of the river back to the countryside centre, thereby adding a further 3½ virtually traffic-

free miles to the ride. This route therefore offers a choice of three distances of between 7 and 15 miles. The nature of this winding valley ensures that you enjoy a new vista at almost every turn that you take, with the fast-flowing river accompanying you below.

BACKGROUND AND PLACES OF INTEREST

Afan Forest Park
This 9,000-acre forest park is situated alongside the A4107 Cwm Afan Scenic Route which links Port Talbot with the high moorland inland. The road was engineered in 1930-2 largely to counteract the unemployment caused by the depression. From the 18th century until fairly recently, the valley was dedicated to coal mining and to industry. A railway was first built in 1859 and linked Swansea Bay with Glyncorrwg for goods only. Later, in 1885, a passenger service was introduced. Although once a coal mining area, it is not very obvious to the uninitiated eye now. In fact, the area is now known by local folk as Little Switzerland, with its steep-sided valley slopes covered with conifers. It is worth noting that in nearby Pontrhydyfen, Richard Burton and Ivor Emmanuel were born. The park has a visitor centre known as the Afan Argoed Countryside Centre. The centrepiece of this is a 'hands on' exhibition that graphically demonstrates the landscape and history of the valley. Nearby is the South Wales Miners Museum, which tells both the technical and social side of mining in the area. Apart from the gentle cycling for potterers described in this chapter, there are also 130 miles of traffic-free tracks providing fairly demanding mountain bike rides in addition to several waymarked walking trails available. Large maps on display boards describe these routes and although there is no cycling leaflet currently available, I understand that this will be addressed soon. The

Left: The South Wales Miners' Museum.

centre is open on a daily basis from April to October and at weekends from November to March (Tel: 01639 850564 for more information).

Margam Country Park

This is very close to the M4, Junction 38. The park originally belonged to Margam Abbey and is now a large recreational area of some 800 acres with a wide choice of attractions, including a visitor centre, waymarked walks, farm trails, deer herds, a classical 18th century orangery, sculpture park and the largest maze in Europe. Within the park sit the ruins of the 13th century Margam Abbey. This is a Cistercian chapter house that is 12-sided outside and circular inside. The park is open daily from April to September and from Wednesdays to Sundays from October to March (Tel: 01639 881635 for more information).

Neath

In common with most settlements in the valleys, Neath has a long industrial background. It was originally a copper centre and boasted the first smelter in Wales, which was built in 1584 by Cornish copper men. Neath Museum has a permanent display which is on show in the Old Mechanics' Institute and a regular visiting exhibition (Tel: 01639 645711 for more details).

ROUTE 24
AFAN FOREST PARK
(A delightful ride along both sides of the Afan Valley)
GLYNCORRWG

Below: The Afan Argoed Countryside Centre.

Starting Point: The ride starts from the car park at the Afan Argoed Countryside Centre.

Parking and Toilets: Park in the Countryside Centre car park where there are toilets.

Distance: 7.2 miles round trip, but extensions of up to 15 miles are possible.

Maps: Ordnance Survey Landranger Sheet 170.

Hills: The only noticeable gradients are the descent and ascent to the footbridge over the river close to the countryside centre.

Surface: The ride on the disused railway track has a mainly compacted dust surface. The ride on the north side of the River Afan has a coarser shingly surface.

Safety: There are no safety hazards on this ride.

Roads and Road Crossings: There is one short section of the ride that is on a quiet road over the bridge in Cymer.

Refreshments: The Wayfarer's Rest is a café at the countryside centre. There is little opportunity for refreshment en route.

Nearest Tourist Information Centre: Old Police Station, John Street, Porthcawl CF36 3DT (Tel: 01656 786639 or 782211).

Cycle Hire: Afan Argoed Cycle Hire (at the countryside centre), Cynonville, Port Talbot (Tel: 01639 850564).

ROUTE INSTRUCTIONS
1. (0 miles): From the centre look for the green sign that denotes the bikepath. Push your bike down the slope paved with slabs, you then run parallel with the A4107 for a short distance and cross under it to join the old railway line. Turn right and head north and you will soon pass through the old Cynonville station.

2. (3.3 miles): The cycleway meets the road in Cymer. Turn left here and then immediately right over the bridge and then left. At this point you will have a choice of taking the cycleway extension to Glyncorrwg or proceeding back along the other side of the river toward Pontrhydyfen (signposted as Pontrhydyfen 6.8km). You soon leave the road and pick up the cycleway.

3. (6.6 miles): Turn sharp left to descend the steep hill to the footbridge by which you can cross the river. Alternatively, you can lengthen the ride by carrying on to Pontrhydyfen and returning on the other side of the river to the countryside centre. Ignore the steps on the other side to go on a little further and then swing left up the hill. You will then meet the outgoing route and will need to pass under the road again to return to the countryside centre.

4. (7.2 miles): Arrive back at the centre.

Below: The Afan Valley.

THE SWANSEA BIKEPATH
SWANSEA TO THE MUMBLES

Above: Swansea's Maritime Quarter.

The town of Swansea would never win a beauty competition, but its people are fortunate because they live within a stone's throw of a perfect paradise — the Gower Peninsula...one of the most exquisite parts of Wales. I went there on a sunny day and found myself in a land of golden gorse, blue butterflies and winds from the sea, H. V. Morton from *In Search of Wales*

This Swansea Bikepath is part of National Cycle Route 4. It is a busy route of 6 miles that follows the coastline around Swansea Bay from the Maritime Quarter to Mumbles using a tarmac path following the line of the earliest ever railway track. There is also a spur running through the Clyne Valley toward Gowerton (which is the subject of Route 26) and a further ride north of Swansea known as the Tawe Riverside Path which uses both banks of the river. Despite its proximity to the second city of Wales, the coastline of Swansea Bay is a surprisingly attractive one. It has clean sandy beaches and distinctive views of Swansea and the Victorian resort of The Mumbles. The City and County of Swansea Council produces a useful leaflet on these bikepaths, which is available from Swansea Tourist Information Office.

BACKGROUND AND PLACES OF INTEREST

Swansea

The Maritime Quarter, which is the starting point for this ride, is an excellent development and has more of a continental feel to it than a British one. The marina basin can berth up to 600 boats and alongside is the home of the Maritime and Industrial Museum together with a good selection of shops, restaurants, pubs and a nightclub. The city centre was completely reconstructed to a new plan after the war, and is spacious and allows for several pedestrian-only streets. In 1700 Swansea could boast of being the largest port in Wales. The smelting industry was attracted to the area by the plentiful coal and many copper works were built. Later, in the 19th century, other smelting industries joined the copper smelters including iron, silver, lead, nickel and tin. It is interesting to learn that Nelson's ships were sheathed in Swansea copper. After 1880, the smelting industry went into decline and the city suffered the wars, the depression and the decline of the coal industry. As you would expect, there are many attractions in Swansea. I will mention only two near the start of the ride. The Maritime and Industrial Museum is concerned with the industry of Swansea and the history of its port and also the history of transport and agriculture of the region. Many interesting boats (including a lightship) are moored alongside in the old South Dock which is now the Marina Main Basin. The Maritime and Industrial Museum is open Tuesdays to Sundays and Bank Holidays (Tel: 01792 650351 for more information). The Swansea Museum, the oldest museum in Wales, is also close to the Maritime Quarter and is traditional rather than trendy. It is concerned with archaeology, natural history and Welsh history. It is also open from Tuesdays to Sundays and Bank Holidays (Tel: 01792 653763 for more information).

The Mumbles

The term 'Mumbles' comes from 'mamelles' which is French for breasts and refers to the two small islands beyond Oystermouth. The name is now applied to the whole promontory which is a popular area, with its pier, lighthouse built in 1793, islands and lifeboat station. It is a charming little Victorian seaside village and a magnificent view of Swansea Bay can be obtained from the 900ft pier. The derivation of Oystermouth is interesting as well, as it is supposedly the nearest that the English tongue can get to pronouncing the Welsh name of Ystumllwynarth. The remains of Oystermouth Castle overlook the 'Mumbles Mile' of pubs and restaurants.

Below: On the Swansea bikepath.

The Gower

The Mumbles is sometimes known as the gateway to the Gower Peninsula — some 15 miles by 8 miles projecting from Swansea into the Bristol Channel. It was the first area in Britain to be designated as an Area of Outstanding Natural Beauty. It is famous for its rugged limestone scenery, golden sands and exposed headlands. In the village of Parkmill is the Gower Heritage Centre which is based around a water-powered corn and saw mill with craft workshops and large tea rooms. The mill was built as long ago as 1160 by the powerful Le Breos family who were Norman rulers of Gower. The waterwheel and grinding machinery are still working and produce flour used in the tea rooms for their bread and cakes. The mill is an example of only 40 left in Wales.

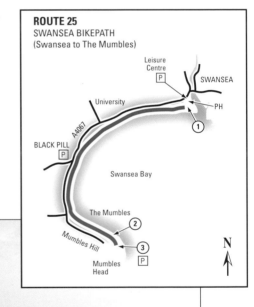

ROUTE 25
SWANSEA BIKEPATH
(Swansea to The Mumbles)

Leisure Centre
P

SWANSEA

University

PH

A4067

BLACK PILL
P

Swansea Bay

The Mumbles

Mumbles Hill

Mumbles Head
P

N

Starting Point: From a car park in the Maritime Quarter.

Parking and Toilets: You will need to park in the Maritime Quarter of Swansea. I parked at the Leisure Centre car park and managed to pick up the Swansea Bikepath fairly easily from there. To leave the car park, you will need to purchase an exit pass from the Leisure Centre. There is also parking at Black Pill and Mumbles Head.

Distance: 12 miles there and back.

Maps: Ordnance Survey Landranger Sheet 159.

Hills: There are no hills.

Surface: Most of the ride is on an old tarmacked railway line, or on the sea wall which is paved in concrete.

Safety: On the sea wall/promenade sections it would be possible for a young child to cycle over the edge and be exposed to a significant drop and nasty consequences. So parents will need to keep a wary eye on young children on these sections.

Roads and Road Crossings: If you wish to carry on to Mumbles Head it is necessary to cycle for a short distance on a quiet little road with a 10mph speed limit.

Refreshments: There are many pubs and restaurants along the 'Mumbles Mile'. There is a large and pleasant café on the sea front at Mumbles.

Nearest Tourist Information Centre: Singleton Street, Swansea SA1 3QG (Tel: 01792 468321).

Cycle Hire: Swansea Cycle Centre, 10 Wyndham Street, Swansea SA1 3HZ (Tel: 01792 410710) and Clyne Valley Cycles, 9 Walters Row, Dunvant SA2 7TB (Tel: 01792 208889).

Above: The Mumbles rocks.

ROUTE INSTRUCTIONS

1. (0 miles): From the Maritime Quarter pick up the bikepath on the foreshore. To do this follow any directions that you may see to The Promenade or The Foreshore.

2. (5.6 miles): Arrive at the Victorian resort of Mumbles. Carry on to Mumbles Head using the quiet little road with the 10mph speed limit.

3. (6.0 miles): Arrive at Mumbles Head.

THE SWANSEA BIKEPATH
SWANSEA TO DUNVANT

'Swansea folk have one peculiarity: they eat a seaweed called laver bread so avidly that they have nearly exhausted local supplies and have to get it from Scotland.' William Condry in *Exploring Wales*

This is a further ride that utilises the Swansea Bikepaths. The early part of the ride is the same as Route 25 but instead of riding to Mumbles we branch off and follow the old LMS railway line up the Clyne Valley, which is a long but hardly perceptible climb up to Dunvant. The start of the route around Swansea Bay is fairly busy with cyclists, but as soon as we enter the Clyne Valley Country Park things become very quiet. The route can be followed as far as Gowerton, and there are plans to extend it to Penclawdd. These bikepaths are a marvellous facility and the City and County of Swansea Council produces a useful leaflet on them, which is available from Swansea Tourist Information Office.

ROUTE 26
SWANSEA BIKEPATH
(Swansea to Dunvant)

③ P DUNVANT

Leisure Centre P
SWANSEA

University A4067

A4118 to
The Gower

PH

①

Clyne Valley Country Park
R. Clyne

② BLACK PILL
P
Swansea Bay

N ↑

BACKGROUND AND PLACES OF INTEREST

The Clyne Valley Country Park
This ride takes you through Clyne Valley Country Park. It is only 3 miles from Swansea city centre and has an abundance of natural and industrial history which can be experienced by the cycle trail or by various walking routes. Nearby, Clyne Gardens are open throughout the year from 8am to dusk. The gardens are nationally famous for the azaleas and rhododendrons and are at their best in May when 'Clyne in Bloom' provides a riot of colour for all to enjoy. At Dunvant there is a memorial to the victims of the Killay Mining Disaster.

The Gower
There are a wealth of ancient sites to visit on Gower. There is Arthur's Stone, a Neolithic tomb on Cefn Bryn, which provides the inspiration for many Arthurian legends associated with Gower. Oxwich Castle is a fortified Tudor manor house that overlooks Oxwich Bay. It is open daily throughout summer with a small entrance fee (Tel: 01222 826174). Weobley Castle is also a fortified manor house and dates mainly from the 13th and 14th centuries and was home to the knightly de la Bere family. It is open throughout the year (Tel: 01222 826174). Finally, Oystermouth Castle, in Mumbles, is open throughout the summer period. Edward I stayed there but now the castle plays host to open-air opera and Shakespeare (Tel: 01792 635444).

Below: Three Cliffs Bay on the Gower Peninsula. *Welsh Tourist Board*

Starting Point: From a car park in the Maritime Quarter.

Parking and Toilets: You will need to park in the Maritime Quarter of Swansea. I parked at the Leisure Centre car park and managed to pick up the Swansea Bikepath fairly easily from there. To leave the car park, you will need to purchase an exit pass from the Leisure Centre. There is also parking at Black Pill.

Distance: 12.4 miles there and back.

Maps: Ordnance Survey Landranger Sheet 159.

Hills: From Black Pill to Dunvant is a long steady climb, but it is not severe and quite within the capability of most people.

Surface: The early part of this ride along the foreshore takes place on a mixture of paving, concrete and tarmac. After branching off on the Clyne Valley spur, the route is mainly tarmac.

Safety: On the sea wall/promenade sections it would be possible for a young child to cycle over the edge and be exposed to a significant drop and nasty consequences. So parents will need to keep a wary eye on young children on these sections.

Roads and Road Crossings: Only one crossing at Black Pill, which is a controlled crossing with traffic lights.

Refreshments: Once you leave Swansea to cycle up the Clyne Valley, there is little opportunity for refreshment, so a picnic at one of the tables provided in the country park is probably the best idea.

Nearest Tourist Information Centre: Singleton Street, Swansea SA1 3QG (Tel: 01792 468321).

Cycle Hire: Swansea Cycle Centre, 10 Wyndham Street, Swansea SA1 3HZ (Tel: 01792 410710) and Clyne Valley Cycles, 9 Walters Row, Dunvant SA2 7TB (Tel: 01792 208889).

ROUTE INSTRUCTIONS

The ride finishes at Dunvant, but if you wish to carry on a little further to Gowerton you could explore north Gower and return on the train from Gowerton to Swansea. However, there is more than one type of train and operator on this route, so you will need to check in advance on carriage of cycles and whether there is a need to make a reservation (Tel: 0345 484950 for the National Rail Enquiry Line).

1. (0 miles): From the Maritime Quarter pick up the bikepath on the foreshore. To do this follow any directions that you may see to The Promenade or The Foreshore.

2. (3.0 miles): At Black Pill, as you reach the trig point at the end of the pitch and putt golf course (this is also where the Clyne River meets the sea), turn right across the pedestrian crossing to enter the Clyne Valley Country Park opposite.

3. (6.2 miles): Although the bikepath goes on to Gowerton, it is very built-up and has no particular attractions, so this ride finishes at Dunvant.

Top: Dunvant.

Above: Memorial to the Killay mining disaster.

🚲 ROUTE 27

CANASTON WOODS
A SHORT EASY FAMILY CYCLE TRAIL

'Here you may look north over the more broken country of the Welsherie springing into the wild sweeps of the Prescelly mountains, or you may face the south and see far over the fatter and smoother country which the English so early made their own.' A. G. Bradley writing on the peculiar contrasts between English and Welsh areas of Pembrokeshire in his *Highways and Byways in South Wales*

Canaston Woods covers 420 acres and is owned by the Forestry Commission. It is a mixture of coniferous woodland and beech edged with oak, ash, hazel and willow. This completely traffic-free ride is on a surfaced cycle trail which utilises 'forest roads' that are only used by the occasional forestry lorry, and a specially constructed section of path. This is an ideal route for families, providing quiet, safe, off-road cycling through mature and attractive woodland. The woods abound with wildlife and I remember being accompanied by the 'honk honk' of the raven

Below: Entrance to Canaston Woods.

and the 'puihu' of the buzzard throughout the whole ride. Although not essential, mountain bikes, or at least bikes with fairly wide tyres, would be preferable on this route. The Canaston Cycle Trails were created by SPARC (the South Pembrokeshire Partnership for Action with Rural Communities) in partnership with the Forestry Commission. A free leaflet on the Canaston Cycle Trails is available from SPARC, Narberth (Tel: 01834 860965).

BACKGROUND AND PLACES OF INTEREST

Canaston Woods
The woods are classed as ancient woodland indicating that they have been in existence for over 300 years. These are the remains of a much larger forest that was at one time an important source of timber for the Slebech Estate. Smaller trees were used for firewood and the larger ones for construction and

ROUTE 27
CANASTON WOODS
(A short easy family cycle trail)

Above: Canaston Woods information board.

shipbuilding. Charcoal was also produced and used to fuel a nearby iron foundry that once existed at Blackpool Mill (see Route 28). In more recent times the sustainable technique of coppicing became the method for ensuring a continuing succession of wood and old examples of this can be seen. Interestingly, Baron de Rutzen of Slebech introduced wild boar into the forest in 1834 for hunting. He also had a plan to introduce wolves, but, needless to say, this was not well liked and was not implemented. You can be assured that you will not meet any wild boar or wolves in Canaston Woods on your ride.

Narberth
Nearby Narberth (originally Castell yn Arberth) is traditionally associated with the Welsh mythological Mabinogion and is a sprawling hilltop town. The origin of the town dates back to a Dark Age castle, and the Vikings plundered here in 994. The connection with the Mabinogion is very well dealt with at the Landsker Visitor Centre (which is combined with a tourist information facility and a local craft shop) and is open daily from April to mid-October, and most weekends from mid-October to March (Tel: 01834 860061 for more information). To the southwest of the town there is a wildfowl centre and country park called Heronsbrook which is very pleasant to visit with ponds, walks, picnic area and rare farm breeds (Tel: 01834 860723).

The Prescelly Hills
This geographical feature suffers from many different spellings, but this is perhaps the most common one. They are the last outcrop of the Cambrian Mountains, that run the length of Wales. It is an open moorland area vaguely reminiscent of parts of Dartmoor due to the rocky outcrops on the hills. The area is of most interest due to the wealth of prehistoric remains in the landscape. Examples are cairns to be found on the hills, and burial chambers, standing stones and stone circles. It is from here that the 'Blue Stones' of Stonehenge are thought to have originated and were taken on their journey down Milford Haven, and up the Bristol Channel.

Above: The waymarking is clear in Canaston Wood.

Starting Point: From the east side of the A4075 at Point 1 on the accompanying map.

Parking and Toilets: Park on the east side of the A4075 where the forest road enters the woods.

Distance: 3 miles round trip.

Maps: Ordnance Survey Landranger Sheet 158.

Hills: This is a very easy ride suitable for young children, with only very short hills.

Surface: Most of this ride is on 'forest roads' which are usually gravelled.

Safety: This is a very safe ride. Keep well clear of any forestry operations that you may come across.

Roads and Road Crossings: None.

Refreshments: There are no refreshments en route. A picnic is strongly recommended.

Nearest Tourist Information Centre: Kingsmoor Common, Kilgetty SA68 0YA (Tel: 01834 814161).

Cycle Hire: Base Camp Llawhaden Bike Hire, Narberth (Tel: 01437 541318). Highgate Cycle Hire, Narberth (Tel 01834 891213).

ROUTE INSTRUCTIONS

1. (0 miles): At the entry point of Canaston Woods from the A4075, take the gravelled forest drive trail straight into the woods as indicated by the green engraved cycle trail sign on the fingerpost.

2. (0.6 miles): You arrive at a clearing in the woods — there is an information point here. Bear right here to follow the green engraved cycle trail sign again.

3. (0.9 miles): Bear off to the left from the gravelled drive to take a lesser used route. Again there is a green engraved cycle trail fingerpost sign here.

4. (1.2 miles): Turn sharp right as indicated by the cycle trail fingerpost sign to descend a steep hill, and across the water splash.

5. (1.3 miles): Turn right at the next cycle trail fingerpost sign.

6. (1.6 miles): You meet the main (gravelled drive) part of the cycle trail again.

7. (2.1 miles): You will meet the point where you turned off the gravelled drive — from here retrace your route back to the car park by the A4075.

8. (3.0 miles): Arrive back at the car park.

LANDSKER OFF-ROAD ROUTE

A CIRCULAR RIDE SOUTHWEST OF NARBERTH

'The distinguishing peculiarity of Pembrokeshire lies of course in its racial composition. The northern half of the county, speaking almost literally, is as Welsh as Cardiganshire in blood and speech. The southern half in both particulars as Hampshire.' A. G. Bradley in his *Highways and Byways in South Wales*

This ride is an adaptation of a ride from the Landsker Cycleways series published by the Greenways Project with assistance from SPARC (the South Pembrokeshire Partnership for Action with Rural Communities) and other local authorities. It is basically an extension of Route 27 (Canaston Woods). Certain sections of this ride become heavily waterlogged at the wetter times of the year, the worst sections being between Point 3 and Point 6. This ride would generally not be suitable for riders under 10 years of age and I would advise that mountain bikes and a mountain biker's mindset (the willingness to become totally covered in mud) are essential during much of the year. A family visiting the area might wish to divide off according to

ability and enthusiasm. Potterers might wish to undertake the alternative Route 27 (Canaston Woods) while the enthusiasts undertake this ride. Two Landsker Cycleways leaflets dealing with local road and off-road routes are available from SPARC at Narberth (Tel: 01834 860965).

BACKGROUND AND PLACES OF INTEREST

Blackpool Mill

The river that flows under Canaston Bridge and past Blackpool Mill is the eastern Cleddau which rises in the Prescelly Mountains. Immediately below the bridge, at Blackpool Mill, the Cleddau meets the highest tides. It is at this point that some historians think that the Prescelly 'blue stones' used to build Stonehenge were launched and then carried down Milford Haven and into the Bristol Channel. The mill itself is a striking building to find in the countryside and has a long history as a flour mill. It was built in 1813 and is one of the finest examples of a water-powered mill in Britain. There is a pleasant two mile walk along the Daugleddau Trail to the remains of a church of the Knights of St John. At Blackpool Mill there is also a shop and a tea room (Tel: 01437 541233). The mill is open daily from Easter to October.

Below: Blackpool Mill.

Fishguard and The Last Invasion

Fishguard is popularly associated with the last mainland invasion of Britain that took place 200 years ago. This was a farcical affair involving three French frigates that arrived off the coast on 22 February 1797 and landed 1,400 convicts. The operation was under the command of an Irish-American General Tate. The local militia gathered rapidly and were quickly successful in defeating the invaders within two days. The incompetent operation was hampered by the drunken state of the convicts who threatened to shoot the General if he did not negotiate for peace, and by the fact that the invaders mistook the red-cloaked Welsh women for British soldiers. Surrender was accepted at the Royal Oak, and at a local church nearby is the grave of Jemima Nicolas who was a cobbler and described to be 'of age 47 and of brawny build and fearsome mien' who captured 14 Frenchmen single handed. She was, not surprisingly, awarded a pension which she drew until she died at the age of 82. There is a leaflet giving details of a 14-mile circuit that visits the sites associated with the invasion and this is available from local Tourist Information Centres.

Below: One of the Landsker route off-road sections.

ROUTE 28
LANDSKER OFF-ROAD ROUTE
(A circular ride southwest of Narberth)

CANASTON BRIDGE A40(T)

① P ⑨

②

A4075

⑧ Dangerous Crossing

NARBE

③ Canaston Wood

④ Cilvoden Farm

⑦

Chapel

⑤ MOLLESTO CROSS

N ↑ ⑥

Starting Point: Start from the car park below.

Parking and Toilets: Park in the small car park by Canaston Bridge at the junction of the A4075 and A40(T).

Distance: 7.1 miles round trip.

Maps: Ordnance Survey Landranger Sheet 158.

Hills: This is an undulating ride with several hills, but none are particularly arduous.

Surface: The surface is a mixture of gravelled forest roads, some tarmac roads and some unsurfaced bridleways that are extremely heavy going in wet weather.

Safety: There are no particular safety hazards on this ride.

Roads and Road Crossings: Extreme care should be taken at Point 3 where the ride crosses the A4075, as this is a fast road with poor visibility. Also, about ³/₄ mile of this ride is on a quiet country road (between Points 6 and 7).

Refreshments: There is a café with home-made lunches and teas at Blackpool Mill.

Nearest Tourist Information Centre: Kingsmoor Common, Kilgetty SA68 0YA (Tel: 01834 814161).

Cycle Hire: Base Camp Hawhaden Bike Hire, Narberth (Tel: 01437 541318). Highgate Cycle Hire, Narberth (Tel 01834 891213).

ROUTE INSTRUCTIONS

1. (0 miles): From the car park, turn right onto the A4075 and take the first right to Blackpool Mill.

2. (0.9 miles): Take the bridleway off to the left up the hill. (The mill and bridge are quite interesting, so it is worth cycling past the bridleway turning to have a look.)

3. (1.5 miles): Cross the A4075 to enter Canaston Wood — immediately take the bridleway to the right as indicated by the red Canaston Trail off-road marker. You will cycle through woodland and then through open land.

4. (2.1 miles): Pass through the first small five-bar wooden gate; there is a red Canaston

Above: One of the several ruined churches in the area.

Trail off-road marker here.

5. (2.2 miles): Avoid the route left indicated by the red Canaston Trail off-road marker sign and carry straight on to follow the blue bridleway sign. There is an interesting small derelict chapel near this point.

6. (3.2 miles): You will meet a surfaced road at Molleston Cross; turn left here.

7. (3.9 miles): Turn left onto the gravelled track that is signposted to Cilvoden Farm. Eventually the surface peters out and the route becomes a trackway.

8. (5.6 miles): You are now back at the point where you originally entered Canaston Wood by the A4075. Retrace your route along the bridleway opposite to return to your starting point via Blackpool Mill.

9. (7.1 miles): Arrive back at Canaston Bridge.

THE BRUNEL CYCLE TRACK
A LINEAR ROUTE ON AN OLD RAILWAY LINE FROM JOHNSTON TO NEYLAND

'The traveller is now well within that compact region known as 'Little England beyond Wales'. Everywhere in the streets of the town, he will hear English spoken...with a kindred strain to that spoken in the heart of England.' A. G. Bradley writing on southwest Pembrokeshire in his *Highways and Byways in South Wales*

This gentle ride is virtually completely traffic-free and takes place on a cycle track that follows an old railway trackbed that was once part of the old GWR (Great Western Railway or as most railway enthusiasts know it — 'God's Wonderful Railway'). The line was originally built by the South Wales Railway which, in 1854, extended its line from Haverfordwest to Neyland where a port for a ferry to Ireland was introduced. The work was finished in August 1855 and in January 1856 a light locomotive completed a trip to Neyland with the great engineer and director of the project, Isambard Kingdom Brunel, on board. The line was closed in 1964 almost exactly 100 years after construction. The cycle route was opened in 1996 and leads you through very green and pleasant countryside and then into the Westfield Pill Nature Reserve and finally the Neyland Marina. A Brunel Cycle Route leaflet is available (20p) from local Tourist Information Centres describing an alternative circular route of 14 miles which is partly on- and off-road. The ride described here, which is on the Brunel Cycle Track, is completely off-road and traffic-free.

BACKGROUND AND PLACES OF INTEREST

Little England Beyond Wales
A glance of a map of south Pembrokeshire tells the story of a successful English colonisation. There are no place names beginning with 'Llan' and 'Aber', instead we

Below: The impressive fortress of Pembroke Castle. *Welsh Tourist Board*

ROUTE 29

THE BRUNEL CYCLE TRACK
(A linear route on an old railway line
from Johnston to Neyland)

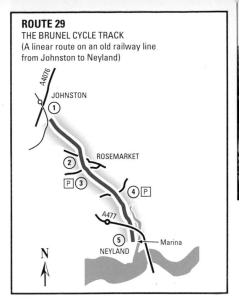

Above: Westfield Pill.

have Jameston, Jeffreyston, Rosemarket, Milford Haven and Haverfordwest. The first language of north Pembrokeshire and Carmarthenshire is Welsh, whereas the language of south Pembrokeshire is firmly English. This has occurred as a result of the influence of the invading Normans together with the later Flemish settlement in the 12th century. The dividing line between these two cultures is the Landsker Line — a line of fortifications and castles built by the Normans to help repel attacks by the native Welsh. This curving line runs from west to east across the centre of the county, and until recent times divided some areas so sharply that the two communities faced each other across the street.

Pembroke

Pembroke Castle is one of the most impressive fortresses in the British Isles, standing as it does on a rocky hill by an inlet of Milford Haven. It was built in the 13th century and it was the centre of power in Pembrokeshire, never being occupied by the Welsh. It is perhaps most famous for one of the longest sieges of the Civil War, but it was eventually taken by Cromwell in July 1648. The Parliamentarians did not carry out their usual degree of damage after capture and although like many old fortifications the stone has been used for local housing, what remains is complete enough to be interesting. The most interesting features are the gatehouse, the round keep and a natural

cavern known as the Wogan Cave. This is reached by a stairway and it opens out on to the river to provide an emergency exit for the castle. Pembroke Castle is open daily between April and October but is closed on Sundays between November and February (Tel: 01646 681510). The town is built within the walls of the old castle and its centre is Main Street which is over 1/2 mile long and has at each end the town's east and west gates. The north gate guards the bridge across the river. The town now revolves around a giant one-way system, part of which is Main Street inside the original town walls, and the other parallel street lies below the walls and provides spacious car parking facilities. Also situated here is the Pembroke Visitor Centre, and this is where any visit to the town should start as Pembroke's past is interestingly brought to life. The Tourist Information Centre also shares the site and it is from here that paths lead you to the old walled town and the castle. Pembroke Visitor Centre is open daily between April and October, and some weekends between November and March (Tel: 01646 622388).

Haverfordwest

Haverfordwest could not be more English. It sits on a hill and would look right in any part of the southwest of England. It is spread below a 13th century castle and is situated on the Western Cleddau. It has several steep streets and attractive Georgian houses. In the 19th century Haverfordwest was a busy port, trading heavily with Bristol and Ireland. The castle has been restored in recent times and houses the Museum and Art Gallery (Open Mondays to Saturdays, Tel: 01437 763708).

Starting Point: This ride starts from the small car park at the beginning of the cycle track. However, there are currently no directions in Johnston to the beginning of the track. From the main road (A4076) in Johnston turn into Langford Road. Cross over the railway line, turn first right and then right into Greenhall Park — a council housing estate.

Parking and Toilets: There is a small car park for about a dozen cars that has been built at the beginning of the cycle track in Greenhall Park. There is also limited parking along the route (see location map) and at Neyland Marina.

Distance: 3.7 miles (7.4 miles there and back).

Maps: Ordnance Survey Landranger Sheet 158.

Hills: There are no significant hills on this ride.

Surface: The type of surface varies from compacted dust to gravel and is generally very good.

Safety: There are no safety hazards.

Roads and Road Crossings: The route crosses a few very minor roads.

Refreshments: There are pubs and restaurants at Neyland Marina.

Nearest Tourist Information Centre: The Guntower, Front Street, Pembroke Dock SA72 6JZ.

Cycle Hire: Mike's Bikes in Haverfordwest (Tel: 01437 760068).

ROUTE INSTRUCTIONS

This is a straightforward ride and few directions are necessary.

1. (0 miles): From the car park join the Brunel Cycle Track.

2. (1.4 miles): Cross a very quiet road.

3. (1.7 miles): Cross a further quiet road — there is also a small car park here.

4. (2.6 miles): Enter the Westfield Pill Nature Reserve. The leaflet seems to discourage cycling through the nature reserve, but the signs by the entrance to the nature reserve confirm that cycling is perfectly permissible. There is also a car park here.

5. (3.7 miles): Having passed under the very high A477 toll bridge you will arrive at the Marina, which marks the end of the Brunel Cycle Track.

Below: The start of the Brunel Cycle Track at Johnston.

Above: Stack Rocks.

THE PEMBROKESHIRE COAST PATH
A RIDE ALONG THE COAST FROM STACK ROCKS TO ST GOVAN'S HEAD

'Homesteads grow scarce and fences fade away into sheep-fed commons as you draw near the brink of somewhat awesome precipices of grey limestone against whose feet the waves rage continuously...' A. G. Bradley writing on his impressions of the coastline near St Govan's Head in his *Highways and Byways in South Wales*

This ride takes advantage of the one part of the Pembrokeshire Coast Path that is a bridleway and therefore provides traffic-free cycling. Starting from Stack Rocks the ride follows the coast path to St Govan's Head and then turns inland on quiet roads for a short distance to Bosherston where there are tea rooms and a good pub. From there we return using the same route. It is important to note that this ride takes place on the Castlemartin Artillery Range which can be closed when firing is in progress. However, the range is not normally active after 5pm and at weekends. Look out for the signs and warning flags. There is a military control point as you leave the B4319 to enter the Castlemartin Range to drive to the car park at St Govan's Head, and there is a notice here indicating whether the range is in use. However, although the range was not in use when I did this ride, certain signs along the route were not indicating the correct state and were contradictory. I would strongly advise that you contact the range office before you start out for the day to ascertain whether there is likely to be any firing that could affect your ride (Tel: 01646 661321).

BACKGROUND AND PLACES OF INTEREST

Bosherston

Bosherston is the destination of our ride and what a perfect one it is, being a picturesque little village with an excellent pub. When we did the ride, although it was September, the weather was gloomy, cold, wet and windy. We stopped at the pub and were almost certainly saved from a severe chill by a beautiful warming bowl of cawl (a nourishing Welsh broth). To complete the picture of Bosherston as the perfect village stop, the large and inviting tea rooms must also be mentioned. Unfortunately, in our condition we could not try both the pub and the tea rooms as we were leaking water everywhere, so we will have to leave it to you to pass judgement on the tea rooms. However, earlier in this century there were three tea rooms in the village plus a further two at St Govan's. Two of the Bosherston ones were next door to each other. Now of course there is only one, but the Olde Worlde Café has been open for tea and cakes for over 70 years. In the early Middle Ages the village was known as Stackpole — the stack being the rock at the entrance to nearby Broad Haven and the pole was the pool or bay. The local manor was owned by William Bosher in the 13th century and the name became Stackpole Bosher and later simply Bosherston (Bosher's settlement). This information is obtained from an interestingly written leaflet by Bosherston Local History Group and Dyfed Archaeological Trust published as a SPARC leaflet.

St Govan's Chapel

This is reached by descending 52 steps from the car park into a steep narrow gully in the cliffs. It is a tiny church blocking a cleft in the rocks that was built for pilgrims visiting the curative well of Govan who was a sixth century monk from Wexford. Much of the stonework is medieval and a probably a replacement of much earlier construction. In the tiny chapel there is a small altar and steps cut into the rock and here there is a fissure which supposedly sheltered St Govan. Today it reputedly grants the wishes of anyone able to turn round inside it without touching the sides. There was at one time a well under the floor, although now dry, which was known for its curative properties.

The Castlemartin Artillery Range

The Castlemartin Artillery Range was created in 1938 as the Royal Artillery Corps Range for the War Department. It took nearly half of the parish of Bosherston. Further land was acquired to the south of the village to extend the range in 1940. These developments meant the disappearance of two farms and nine dwellings. The coastline hereabouts boasts some of the finest cliffs in Britain. Stack Rocks at the start of the ride are more properly known as Elegug Stacks (elegug being Welsh for guillemot.) These rocks are reputedly magnificent in spring when the guillemots, razorbills and kittiwakes are massed for breeding.

Below: St Govan's Chapel.

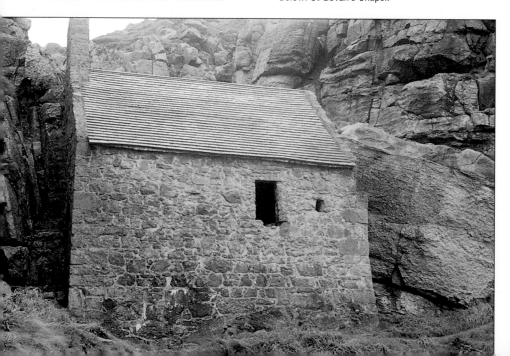

Above: Military range sign.

Starting Point: This ride starts from the car park at Stack Rocks.

Parking and Toilets: Park at the car park at Stack Rocks. There is also parking at St Govan's Head and at the end of the ride at Bosherston.

Distance: 4.6 miles (9.2 miles there and back).

Maps: Ordnance Survey Landranger Sheet 158.

Hills: There are no significant hills on this ride.

Surface: The clifftop ride is on a shingly surface and tends to be a little rough, so a mountain bike is probably preferable.

Safety: Parents should bear in mind that this is a clifftop ride, although the route generally keeps safely away from the cliff edge. Also, being a firing range, it is important to keep to the route and not touch any suspicious looking objects.

Roads and Road Crossings: The section from St Govan's Head to Bosherston is on a quiet country road.

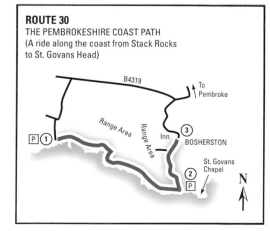

Refreshments: A good choice of refreshments exists in Bosherston at the village tea rooms and at St Govan's Inn. The inn is a haunt of coastal climbers and there are many photographs of climbers in action around the local coastline. There is also a notebook on the bar to record newly discovered ways of climbing particular cliffs.

Nearest Tourist Information Centre: The Visitor Centre, Commons Road, Pembroke SA71 4EA (Tel: 01646 622388).

Cycle Hire: Bro Bikes, Tenby (Tel: 01834 811100). Tenby Cycle Hire, Tenby (01834 845955).

ROUTE INSTRUCTIONS
The route is very straightforward and simply follows the coast around to St Govan's Head and the chapel and then uses a country road to Bosherston.

1. (0 miles): From the Stack Rocks car park, pass through the gate and take the shingly path to head east along the bridleway which is initially grassy but then becomes shingly.

2. (3.1 miles): Arrive at the St Govan's Chapel car park. Pass the control point and take the country road to Bosherston.

3. (4.6 miles): Arrive in Bosherston.

ROUTE 30
THE PEMBROKESHIRE COAST PATH
(A ride along the coast from Stack Rocks to St. Govans Head)

FORESTRY COMMISSION LAND

The Forestry Commission (FC) was established in 1919 to ensure an adequate supply of timber for the nation's needs. At the time it was considered that the long period of time between planting and felling made this an unsuitable matter to entrust to the response of free enterprise to supply and demand. It is the largest landowner in the United Kingdom. It owns holdings of over two million acres and advises private owners on the management of a further million acres. In Wales in particular, it owns 7% of the land area — approximately 327,000 acres.

Many areas of woodland owned or managed by the Forestry Commission have gravelled roads. These are well-engineered routes originally intended to enable timber removal by large lorries. However, for the majority of the time these roads are not in active use and offer considerable scope for peaceful traffic-free enjoyment by the cyclist. When you are in forested areas you will see many references to 'Forest Enterprise'. This is an executive agency of the Forestry Commission that manages the forest estate.

Of course there are a great number of public rights of way on land owned or managed by the Forestry Commission and you have an inalienable right to cycle on bridleways, BOATs (Byways Open to All Traffic) and RUPPs (Roads Used as Public Paths) irrespective of who is the landowner. You must of course give way to horses and walkers on bridleways. Cycling on routes other than public rights of way can be done provided that the Forestry Commission has given permission — these routes are therefore known as permissive routes. A permissive route only exists while the landowner gives permission for use, which can in theory be withdrawn at any time.

Generally, the enlightened view of the Forestry Commission is that cycling is consistent with the use of forests for quiet enjoyment and therefore its policy is to allow cycling unless public access is restricted by title conditions or forestry operations. The precise situation will vary in each piece of woodland depending on such things as whether the commission owns the land or leases it, the existence of sporting rights, the size of the woodland block and the nature of the subsoil. The situation is therefore one of a delicate balance between forestry needs, sporting needs, riding, walking and cycling.

The general rule is that you may cycle on public rights of way (except footpaths). You may also cycle on the forestry roads provided there is no sign restricting public access — for example, for sporting reasons or forestry operations — or

specifically restricting cycling on, for example, a walkers' trail. An increasing number of forest areas have waymarked trails for cyclists to use. Basically, if you use your common sense, and follow the cycle code then you will be welcomed by the Forestry Commission.

THE CYCLE CODE IS:

- Expect the unexpected. Keep your speed down.
- Remember other vehicles use forest roads as well as you!
- Give way to walkers — be friendly towards other forest users.
- Hail a horse and avoid an accident!
- Keep away from all forest operations.
- Do not pass any vehicles loading timber until you have been told to do so.
- Footpaths are for walkers only!
- Cycle with care and you can come back again!

Forest Enterprise produces some helpful and informative leaflets about leisure opportunities in general, and cycling in particular, in Wales. These are:

- *Cycling in the Forest — Great Britain*. A guide to all of the off-road cycling locations in the forests of Britain.
- *Forests of Wales*. A guide to the leisure opportunities available at 15 Forest Enterprise sites in Wales, together with their locations.
- *Forests of North Wales*. A guide to the leisure opportunities available in the woodlands of Snowdonia, Anglesey, the northeast, the west and mid-Wales, together with their locations.
- *Forests of South Wales*. A guide to the leisure opportunities available in the woodlands of south Wales.

It is fairly rare for me to become lost, but when I do it is always in woodland. There are usually no distinct landmarks by which you can navigate and it is less easy to sight the sun which also makes navigation difficult. So a little care is needed in the larger areas of woodland if you are not to run the risk of becoming totally disorientated. I would suggest that if you intend to explore a particular area of woodland and wish to plan a route using gravelled roads, then you should either obtain a detailed leaflet from Forest Enterprise — there is usually one available from the relevant visitor centre or local Forest Enterprise office — or alternatively buy the 1:25,000 scale Ordnance Survey Explorer, Outdoor Leisure or Pathfinder map for the area.

SNOWDONIA NATIONAL PARK
(NP1 ON LOCATION MAP)

The Snowdonia National Park Authority produces a couple of leaflets providing information. The off-road cycling situation can currently be summarised as access by right of way only, with a voluntary agreement to restrict the high level of use of the bridleways to the summit of Snowdon. This agreement states that there should be no cycling on Snowdon bridleways between 1 June and 30 September between 10am and 5pm. Outside of this there is no restriction. Leaflets available are:

- *Off Road Cycling in Snowdonia*. This provides general advice and codes of conduct.
- *National Voluntary Agreement Snowdonia*. A guide to those bridleways where the agreement applies.

BRECON BEACONS NATIONAL PARK
(NP2 ON LOCATION MAP)

Off-road access by cycle is by right of way only. The Taff Trail is an important route and the most scenic stretches of this long-distance cycle route are contained within the national park. The Taff Trail is covered in detail in Routes 20 to 23.

PEMBROKESHIRE COAST NATIONAL PARK (NP3 ON LOCATION MAP)

Due to the topography of the national park, opportunities for off-road cycling are limited and rely on the availability of bridleways and green lanes. Some leaflets have been produced by SPARC and details are listed in the chapter entitled *'Routes Described in Local Authority Leaflets'*.

WATER COMPANIES

Although there are 91 reservoirs owned by Welsh Water in Wales, opportunities for cycling reservoirs in Wales are limited and most of the possibilities are covered in the detailed routes in this book. Further information can be found in *A guide to recreation around the reservoirs of Wales* published by Welsh Water.

FORESTRY COMMISSION SITES WITH OPPORTUNITIES FOR TRAFFIC-FREE CYCLING

The main sites of activity are listed here, but it is not an all-inclusive list and further additions are likely to be made in the future:

North Wales: *FC1 Gwydyr Forest Park*. There are two well-waymarked traffic-free cycle trails on undulating forest tracks. One of them is featured in Route 4. A leaflet is available from the Tourist Information Centre in Betws-y-coed (Tel: 01690 710426).

Mid Wales: *FC2 Coed y Brenin Forest Park*. This is arguably the mountain biking centre of Wales. There are a number of well-waymarked traffic-free cycle trails available — the 'Red Bull' Route, the 'Karimoor' Route, the 'Expert' Route, the 'Sport' Route and the 'Fun' Route. Beginners should content themselves with the 'Fun Route' which has some short cut options. Leaflets are available from the visitor centre (Tel: 01341 422289).

Southwest Wales: *FC3 Brechfa Forest*. There are three fully waymarked mountain bike routes and a 7-mile family cycling trail. A leaflet is available from Forest Enterprise, Llanymddyfri Forest District Office (Tel: 01550 720394).

Southeast Wales: *FC4 Garwnant Forest*. A leaflet called Garwnant Forest Routes which covers both walking and cycling routes is available from the Garwnant Forest Centre at Merthyr Tydfil (Tel: 01685 723060). *FC5 Afan Forest Park*. There is a family cycle trail along a disused railway line, a mountain bike trail and 130 miles of forest tracks to explore (Tel: 01639 850564).

ROUTES DESCRIBED IN LOCAL AUTHORITY LEAFLETS

This section describes the cycle routes published by the unitary authorities and other local organisations in Wales at the time of writing. The range of leaflets is developing all the time and may not be absolutely complete. Also included, where known, are planned routes under development or for which funding is awaited. Many of the routes listed below are not traffic-free but take you along quiet country lanes. If the existence of a leaflet is indicated it is free unless otherwise stated.

CAERPHILLY

Sirhowy Valley Country Park. A free map and guide on a low level cycle ride and two mountain bike rides. Available from the country park (Tel: 01495 270991).

CEREDIGION

Nant yr Arian Forest Map. A walkers' map but it gives a useful insight into the forest tracks. Available from Forest Enterprise, Nant yr Arian, Aberystwyth (Tel: 01974 261404).

CONWY

Conwy Valley Cycle Route. Leaflet outlines two signposted routes of 21 to 25 miles. Available from Conwy County Borough Council, Colwyn Bay (Tel: 01492 574000).

DENBIGHSHIRE

Vale of Clwyd — A Scenic Route for Cycling. A 35-mile route on quiet country roads through the Clwyd Valley. Available from Highways and Transportation Department, Caledfryn, Smithfield Road, Denbigh, Denbighshire LL16 3RJ (Tel: 01824 706000).

Denbighshire Council also currently has a number of off-road cycle route initiatives at various stages of maturity:
The Prestatyn/Dyserth Way. A short route along a disused railway line.
The Denbighshire section of the National Cycle Network, which will run along the Denbighshire coast.
The Vale of Clwyd Route, which will run from Rhyl to Cynwyd
Off Road Mountain Bike Routes in Denbighshire. Three routes are under preparation.

Llyn Brenig Visitor Map. A trail map for walkers and cyclists showing a route around the reservoir. Available from Llyn Brenig Visitor Centre, Cerrigydrudion, Ruthin (Tel: 01490 420463).

GWYNEDD

Lonydd Glas Gwynedd Recreational Routes. A well-produced leaflet providing details of three traffic-free recreational routes which have been established on old railway lines. Available from Planning and Economic Development Department, Gwynedd Council, Council Offices, Caernarfon, Gwynedd LL55 1SH (Tel: 01286 672255).

Maentwrog Woodlands. A leaflet showing walking and cycling routes close to the Ffestiniog Railway. Available from local TICs.

ISLE OF ANGLESEY

Rural Cycling on Anglesey. A well-produced leaflet with detailed directions and mapping for four fully signposted cycling tours with possible distances of 11 to 22 miles. Available from Highways and Technical Services Department, Isle of Anglesey County Council, Llangefni, Anglesey LL77 7TW (Tel: 01248 752300).

PEMBROKESHIRE

The Brunel Cycle Route. A 14-mile circular cycle route that explores the Daugleddau Estuary using quiet country lanes, bridleways and an old railway line. Published by Menter Preseli and available from local TICs.

Landsker Cycleways — Road Routes. Ninety-five miles on quiet country lanes in South

Pembrokeshire with day route links which can be used to form circular routes of between 28 and 41 miles, with each one capable of being started from a railway station. Published by the Greenways Project with assistance from several local agencies, and available from SPARC, The Old School, Station Road, Narberth, Pembrokeshire SA67 7DU (Tel: 01834 860965).

Landsker Cycleways — Off Road Routes. Two circular routes centred on Narberth and Pembroke with distances of 12 to 21 miles and significant off-road elements. Published by the Greenways Project with assistance from several local agencies, and available from SPARC, The Old School, Station Road, Narberth, Pembrokeshire SA67 7DU (Tel: 01834 860965).

Canaston Cycle Trails, Short easy trails on forest tracks. Available from SPARC, The Old School, Station Road, Narberth, Pembrokeshire SA67 7DU (Tel: 01834 860965).

The Last Invasion Trail Fishguard. Fourteen-mile circuit visiting the sites associated with the abortive French invasion of 1797. Available from local TICs.

Rail 'n' Ride, Leaflets giving seven off-road routes from Narberth and nearby railway stations. Send SAE to D. Brown, 16 Lady Park, Tenby, SA70 8HJ.

Lyn Lech Owain Country Park. Leaflet and maps showing walks and cycle route. Available from local TICs.

Pembrey Country Park. Leaflet and map showing cycle track and other facilities. Available from Country Park, Pembrey, Llanelli (Tel: 01554 833913).

POWYS

The Elan Trail. A leaflet is planned for publication in early 1999 (see Route 14). This will be available from Technical Services Department, Powys County Council, County Hall, Llandrindod Wells, Powys LD1 5LG (Tel: 01597 826000).

The Kerry Ridgeway. A leaflet has been produced on this route by Powys County Council. It is intended for walkers but is also a useful guide if you are cycling. Send SAE plus extra 20p stamp to Llandrindod Wells TIC (Tel: 01597 822600).

RHONDDA CYNON TAFF

Rhondda Community Route (Ringway Walking and Mountain Bike Route). A 6-mile route around the Rhondda Valley. Available from Valleys Forest Initiative Recreation Ranger (Tel: 01639 850564).

SWANSEA

Swansea Bikepaths. Information on three traffic-free cycle paths around Swansea. Available from Swansea TIC, Singleton Street, Swansea SA1 3QG (Tel: 01793 468321).

Cycling in and around Swansea. Twenty-one cycle routes mostly on local roads but some traffic-free. Available from Swansea TIC, Singleton Street, Swansea SA1 3QG (Tel: 01793 468321).

Mountain Biking on the Gower Peninsula. Describes a hilly 22-mile route using the western bridleways of Gower. Send SAE to CTC Offroad, Parc Mowlais, Llangannoch, Llanelli SA14 8XZ.

In the Saddle. Cycling and Horse Riding in the Bridgend area. Available from Sarn TIC (Tel: 01656 654906) or Porthcawl TIC (Tel: 01656 786639/782211).

LEAFLETS COVERING MORE THAN ONE AUTHORITY'S AREA

Cycling Wales 1998, An excellent full colour 56-page booklet providing details on cycle routes, cycling publications, cycling breaks and tours and accommodation throughout Wales. Available from TICs throughout Wales.

The Taff Trail. A fully illustrated A2-size leaflet with map and colour photographs. Available from TIC's or the Taff Trail Project, Groundwork Merthyr & Rhondda Cynon Taff, Fedw Hir, Llwydcoed, Aberdare CF44 0DX (Tel: 01685 883880).

The Taff Trail. A set of six inexpensive leaflets describing the route in detail. Enquire for cost and p&p details from local TIC's or the Taff Trail Project, Groundwork Merthyr & Rhondda Cynon Taff, Fedw Hir, Llwydcoed, Aberdare CF44 0DX (Tel: 01685 883880).

The Celtic Trail (also known as the South Wales Cycleway). This is a 186-mile route from Newport to Kidwelly currently under development as Route 4 of the National Cycle network. An advance leaflet describing the proposed route is available from Groundwork Cymru Wales, Mynyddislwyn Offices, Bryn Road, Pontllanfraith, Blackwood, Gwent NP2 2BF (Tel: 01495 222605).

Below:
The start of the Taff Trail ride in the Afan Forest Park.

In Wales, the local unitary authority is a good starting point to find out the local cycle routes in a particular area. There are 22 of these and the area covered by each one varies enormously. Powys County Council, for example, covers a huge area but some of the authorities in the Valleys, although they may represent a high population and have many cycling opportunities, are physically very small (Merthyr Tydfil and Bridgend for example). The particular department that deals with cycling promotion also varies from council to council. Often it is the technical services department, but it can be economic development or tourism. In general, I have quoted the department that responded to my enquiries.

BLAENAU GWENT
Director of Engineering, Blaenau Gwent County Borough Council, Municipal Offices, Civic Centre, Ebbw Vale NP3 6XB (Tel: 01495 350555).

BRIDGEND
Highways and Technical Services, Bridgend County Borough Council, Civic Offices, Angel Street, Bridgend CF31 1LX (Tel: 01656 643643).

CAERPHILLY
Directorate of Technical Services, Caerphilly County Borough Council, Council Offices, Pontllanfraith, Blackwood NP2 2YW (Tel: 01495 235311).

CARDIFF
Director of Highway and Transportation Services, Cardiff County Council, County Hall, Atlantic Wharf, Cardiff CF1 5UW (Tel: 01222 872000).

CEREDIGION
Highways Property and Works Department, Ceredigion County Council, County Hall, Market Street, Aberaeron SA46 0AT (Tel: 01545 570382).

CARMARTHENSHIRE
Transportation and Engineering Department, Carmarthenshire County Council, Llanstephan Road, Johnstown, Carmarthen SA31 3LZ (Tel: 01267 234567).

CONWY
Technical Services Department, Conwy County Council, Civic Offices, Colwyn Bay LL29 8AR (Tel: 01492 574000).

DENBIGHSHIRE
Highways and Transportation Department, Denbighshire County Council, Caledfryn, Smithfield Road, Denbigh, Denbighshire LL16 3RJ (Tel: 01824 706000).

FLINTSHIRE
Highways Transportation and Engineering Department, Flintshire County Council, County Hall, Mold CH7 6NF (Tel: 01352 752121).

GWYNEDD
Planning and Economic Development Department, Gwynedd Council, Caernarfon, Gwynedd LL55 1SH (Tel: 01286 672255).

ISLE OF ANGLESEY
Highways and Technical Services Department, Isle of Anglesey County Council, Llangefni, Anglesey LL77 7TW (Tel: 01248 752300).

MERTHYR TYDFIL
Technical Services Department, Merthyr Tydfil County Borough Council, Ty Keir Hardie, Riverside Court, Avenue De Clichy, Merthyr Tydfil CF47 8XF (Tel: 01685 726233).

MONMOUTHSHIRE
Engineering Department, Monmouthshire County Council, County Hall, Cwmbran NP44 2XH (Tel: 01633 838838).

NEATH PORT TALBOT
Technical and Property Services Department, Neath Port Talbot County Borough Council, Civic Centre, Penllergaer SA4 1GH (Tel: 01639 763333).

NEWPORT
Director of Development and Transportation, Newport County Borough Council, Civic Centre, Newport NP9 4UR (Tel: 01633 244491).

PEMBROKESHIRE
Transportation and Technical Services Department, Pembrokeshire County Council, Cambria House, Haverfordwest, Pembrokeshire SA71 1TP (Tel: 01437 764551).

POWYS
Highways and Property Directorate, Powys County Council, County Hall, Llandrindod Wells, Powys LD1 5LG (Tel: 01597 826605).

RHONDDA CYNON TAFF
Development Planning and Environment Department, Rhondda Cynon Taff County Borough Council, The Grange, Tyfica Road, Pontypridd CF37 2DD (Tel: 01443 484400).

SWANSEA
Planning Department, City and County of Swansea, The Guildhall, Swansea SA1 4PH (Tel: 01792 635010).

TORFAEN
Director of Development, Torfaen County Borough Council, County Hall, Cwmbran, Torfaen NP44 2WN (Tel: 01495 762200).

VALE OF GLAMORGAN
Directorate of Economic Development, Planning, Transportation and Highways, Vale of Glamorgan Council, Dock Office, Barry Docks, Barry CF63 4RT (Tel: 01446 704600).

Above: One of the off-road sections on the Landsker Cycleways.

WREXHAM
Transportation and Engineering Department, Wrexham County Borough Council, Crown Buildings, PO Box 1293, Wrexham LL11 1WQ (Tel: 01978 297100).

BRITISH WATERWAYS
For Llangollen & Montgomery Canal: Canal Office, Birch Road, Ellesmere, Shropshire SY12 9AA (Tel: 01691 622549).

For Monmouthshire & Brecon Canal, Swansea Canal: The Wharf, Govilon, Abergavenny, Monmouthshire NP7 9NY (Tel: 01873 830328).

CYCLISTS TOURING CLUB (CTC)
Cotterell House, 69 Meadrow, Godalming, Surrey GU7 3HS (Tel: 01483 417217).
The CTC is Britain's national cyclists' association and works for all cyclists. It provides advice, legal aid and insurance, and campaigns to improve facilities and opportunities for cyclists. It publishes a very useful guide to the cycle routes in England, Wales, Scotland and Ireland which is regularly updated.

GREATER GWENT CYCLING CONSORTIUM
c/o Monmouthshire County Council, County Hall, Cwmbran NP44 2XH (Tel: 01633 644853).
Development of cycling routes in Blaenau Gwent, Monmouthshire and Torfaen, with Sustrans.

GROUNDWORK CYMRU WALES
Mynyddislwyn Offices, Bryn Road, Pontllanfraith, Blackwood, Gwent NP2 2BF (Tel: 01495 222605).
Responsible for the development of the Celtic Trail.

GROUNDWORK MERTHYR AND RHONDDA CYNON TAFF
Fedw Hir, Llwydcoed, Aberdare CF44 0DX (Tel: 01685 883880).
Responsible for development of the Taff Trail.

SUSTRANS
35 King Street, Bristol BS1 4DZ (Tel: 0117 926 8893).
Sustrans is a national charity that designs and builds traffic-free routes for cyclists, pedestrians and disabled people. It is promoting the National Cycle Network which will comprise over 6,500 miles in the four home countries, and is scheduled to be complete by 2005.

WALES TOURIST BOARD
Brunel House, 2 Fitzalan Road, Cardiff CF2 1UY (Tel: 01222 499909).